PRAYING TOGETHER
FOR
TRUE
REVIVAL

Jonathan Edwards for Today's Reader

T. M. MOORE, SERIES EDITOR

Also in this series:
Growing in God's Spirit

PRAYING TOGETHER
FOR
TRUE
REVIVAL

JONATHAN
EDWARDS

EDITED *by* T. M. MOORE

INTRODUCTION *by*
JOHN H. ARMSTRONG

FOREWORD *by*
ERWIN W. LUTZER

P&R
PUBLISHING
P.O. BOX 817 • PHILLIPSBURG • NEW JERSEY 08865-0817

Page design by Tobias Design
Typesetting by Lakeside Design Plus

Printed in the United States of America

Library of Congress Cataloging-in-Publication Data
Edwards, Jonathan, 1703–1758.
    [Humble attempt]
    Praying together for true revival / Jonathan Edwards ; edited by T. M. Moore ; introduction by John H. Armstrong ; foreword by Erwin W. Lutzer.
        p. cm.—(Jonathan Edwards for today's reader)
    Includes index.
    ISBN 0-87552-624-1 (paper)
    1. Church—Unity—Early works to 1800. 2. Prayer—Early works to 1800. 3. Eschatology—Early works to 1800. I. Moore, T. M. (Terry Michael), 1949– II. Title.

BX8.3.E39 2004
269—dc22

                                                    2004044159

To

James A. R. Johnson

CONTENTS

SERIES INTRODUCTION

Jonathan Edwards (1703–1758) is one of the great figures of American church history. Pastor, theologian, evangelist, missionary, husband, and father, Edwards was mightily used of God in his day, and his written works continue to instruct and nurture those who take the time to study them in our own. During his tenure as pastor in the Congregational church in Northampton, Massachusetts, Edwards's preaching was the catalyst God's Spirit used to ignite two powerful seasons of revival, including the Great Awakening of the 1740s. He was a man of the Book and a man of the church, devoting himself to the study of God's Word and the work of pastoral care and edification in congregations in New York City, Northampton, and Stockbridge, Massachusetts, where he served as a missionary to Native Americans. Although he was elected president of Princeton College in 1757, his untimely death made his tenure there all too brief.

This series is devoted to bringing the sermons and other works of Jonathan Edwards to today's readers in a form that can make for careful reading, thoughtful consideration, lively discussion, and significant growth in the grace and knowledge of the Lord. Edwards preached to farmers and merchants, homemakers and youth, Native

Americans and small-town professionals. Although his language can seem at times obscure and the logic of his arguments demands our diligent attention, the ordinary people of his day understood him quite well. For nearly three hundred years the works of Jonathan Edwards have instructed and inspired pastors, theologians, and lay readers to a greater love of God and more diligence in spreading God's love to others. This suggests that Edwards's works can serve us in our generation as well.

Edwards's sermons and books are steeped in Scripture and employ careful exposition and rigorous logic to make the glory of the gospel of Jesus Christ clear and compelling. His was indeed a "rational Biblical theology," to borrow a phrase from Dr. John Gerstner, to whom contemporary Christians owe a great debt for his tireless promotion and exposition of the works of the greatest theologian ever to grace the American ecclesiastical scene. For a variety of reasons—among them the demanding nature of Edwards's writing, his use, at times, of archaic or unfamiliar terms, and the difficulty of procuring his works—contemporary readers have not availed themselves of Edwards's sermons and books as much as they might. To their enormous credit, the editors and publishers of the Banner of Truth Trust have labored to overcome these difficulties by making a large number of Edwards's works available in two hefty volumes and by publishing individual sermons and books as separate publications. We are grateful to the Trust for granting us permission to use the edition of Edwards's works prepared by Edward Hickman, first published in 1834 and kept in print by Banner since 1974, for the texts in this series.

The books in this series present the works of Edwards in their original form, as prepared by Hickman, without significant modification in his language. At times we have updated the spelling of a word, altered punctuation, or included Scripture references that Edwards omitted in his texts. We have added headings and subheadings to clarify his arguments, divided some long paragraphs, and portioned each work into short chapters to allow for more careful and considerate reading. We have also incorporated study questions at the end of each chapter to promote thoughtful reflection on the meaning and application of Edwards's arguments and to encourage use of his works in reading and discussion groups.

This series is prepared under the sponsorship of the Jonathan Edwards Institute, whose mission—to promote and nurture a God-entranced worldview—mirrors that of Edwards. We are grateful to Allan Fisher and the staff of P&R Publishing for their vision for and commitment to the plan and purposes of this series. Our hope is that the books in this series will introduce Jonathan Edwards to a new generation of readers and draw them more deeply and passionately into the knowledge of God. We offer them with the hope that God, who sent the Spirit of revival to his church in Edwards's day, might be pleased to use this series as he moves to revive, renew, and restore his glory in his Bride once again.

T. M. Moore
The Jonathan Edwards Institute

❊ ❊ ❊

A series of volumes dedicated to the memory of one of whom many people are unaware needs some explanation. Yet those who have known Jim Johnson understand at once why an exploration of the thought of Jonathan Edwards is a fitting tribute.

Jim was a husband to Martha and father to three sons, Mark, Steve, and David, who are dedicated followers of Christ. He was the mentor and encourager of untold numbers of young men in every walk of life and served as an elder in his church, the Fourth Presbyterian Church in Bethesda, Maryland.

Jim possessed many intellectual qualifications. He was trained in the liberal arts, and he possessed a doctoral degree in jurisprudence. Far from living in academic isolation, he also held various positions within American corporate life, and he worked and moved with ease in government.

He was fully aware of the reality of the fallenness of our humanity. He lived with it and experienced some of its harshest dealings. Yet to each of his callings, and in all his experiences, Jim brought a devotion to Christ and a love of truth. He was an example of one who sought to bring all of life captive to the Word of God.

Jim Johnson serves as a model to those who seek to harness a vital, living relationship with Christ with an honest pursuit of working that out with theological integrity and ethical rigor. When faced with the diagnosis of inoperable cancer, he showed that, as Jonathan Edwards often re-marked, Christians can die well. Like Edwards's faith, Jim's was real, true, and practical, and it demanded to be worked out in intellectual, experiential, and ethical ways.

Redeemed by Christ, Jim lived life in gratitude, which is why each one of us who knew him mourned the passing of a great encourager, a powerful mentor, and a humble servant of the Lamb.

Robert M. Norris, senior pastor
Fourth Presbyterian Church
Bethesda, Maryland

Foreword

You are holding in your hands a book that should be read by every Christian who is concerned about the state of the church in America in the twenty-first century. If you are a pastor, you will especially find this work to be of profound importance. And if you believe, with me, that focused, earnest, and definite prayer languishes in our churches, then you too should read it, even if you are not a pastor. This is unadulterated high-octane spiritual fuel designed for a season of uncommon and serious prayer, which would likely precede a real revival. Who can argue with such an agenda in such morally dark times?

When I read Jonathan Edwards's *An Humble Attempt,* the traditional short title by which this work is known, faith was birthed in my heart; faith that in response to focused and united prayer, God might yet do a mighty work in our day. For decades I have believed that the church in the West needs a true revival. I even wrote an account of revival in Saskatchewan, Canada, in the early 1970s. I have longed and prayed for "showers of blessing" on many occasions since I undertook that study. In reading this book I have come to see afresh how the sovereign purposes of God are uniquely connected to the extraordinary and united prayer of God's people.

Jonathan Edwards had a different understanding of the millennium than many in our day, including me, but I still urge you to read him. Don't let his particular view of Revelation 20 detract you from the great burden of his heart. His passion and clear instruction on how concerts of prayer can be mobilized for the renewal of the church and, above all, for the recovery of the glory of God among us is something we desperately need.

The historical introduction by my friend John Armstrong sets a context for the book and clearly shows how it can profit modern readers. Read it carefully, and then let Edwards's arguments wash over you with deep prayer. This just may be the kindling for the fires of true revival that you and I need. Whether you know much about Jonathan Edwards, or even very little, this book is a great place to soak your mind and heart in the great truths of biblical revival and the insightful writing of the famous American theologian Jonathan Edwards.

You rarely hear it said, at least these days, that prayerlessness is a great sin. According to the Scriptures spiritual apathy, and the consequent sin of prayerlessness, is most often connected to God's discipline of his people. If we would see the heavens opened, with new refreshing mercies of grace, then we, the people of God, must seek his face and call upon him in humble united prayer.

John Armstrong tells us in his introduction that Edwards's book is the "classic" on the relationship between prayer and true revival. I agree with him. If you prayerfully read these pages, the ripples of blessing just might go to "the edge of the pond" and then drift on to "eternity."

Erwin W. Lutzer, pastor
Moody Church, Chicago

INTRODUCTION

I think I can safely say that the little book you now hold in your hands has done more to spark prayer for true revival than any other book in human history, besides the Holy Scriptures. It has generally been understood that a classic is a book judged to be of highest quality over a significant period of time. By this definition, this book is undoubtedly *the* classic work on the connection of extraordinary prayer to seasons of awakening.

Jonathan Edwards, who is often thought of as one of America's greatest philosopher-theologians, was above all a devout Christian who saturated himself in the Word of God. He was taught the truths of the Reformed faith and the practice of Puritan piety from his childhood. A graduate of Yale College (1720) at the ripe old age of seventeen, he became a pastor in New York City in August 1722, shortly before his twentieth birthday. By the age of twenty-one he was a tutor at Yale, and in 1726 he became an associate minister to his famous maternal grandfather, Solomon Stoddard. It was there, in Northampton, Massachusetts, that he saw the fruit of past local revivals firsthand and learned that the Spirit was often poured out in copious showers of blessing upon the church.

When Stoddard died in 1729, Edwards became the minister of the Congregational church, where he served until a tragic dismissal in 1750. In the later years of his life Edwards was pastor of a mission church of Native Americans in Stockbridge, which was then the frontier of western Massachusetts. He left Stockbridge in February 1757 to become the second president of the College of New Jersey (later to become Princeton). One week after arriving in Princeton he was inoculated against smallpox and less than a month later died of the dreaded disease. He is buried, alongside his beloved wife, Sarah, in the cemetery just across the street from Princeton University.

The written corpus of Jonathan Edwards is of several types. Early in his career he began to publish sermons and occasional pieces. This continued until he died. His private notebooks and personal writings soon followed. (Some of these written pieces, called "Miscellanies," are just now appearing in large academic volumes published by Yale University Press.) His philosophical and theological books, written in the latter part of his life, are perhaps the best known of his written works.

Most students of Jonathan Edwards agree that the most notable of his occasional writings, at least in his lifetime, dealt with revival. It was during the years of 1734–1735 that he witnessed a great outpouring of the Spirit of God upon the people of Northampton. Initially the work of revival began when a woman came under conviction of sin and estrangement from Christ upon hearing sermons on justification by faith alone. Her conversion sparked an extraordinary work of the Holy Spirit that resulted in several hundred conversions (a huge number in a town of little more than one thousand people). The zeal of this movement spread to other towns in the Connecticut River Valley and waves of fresh revival were the result. Accounts of these events, written by Edwards, were then sent to Boston. From there they reached across the colonies and eventually back to Great Britain. This movement of revival subsided in 1735, but in the fall of 1740, when the famous itinerant George Whitefield came to New England, the Spirit again moved with great effect. Whitefield paid an eventful visit to Northampton in the fall of 1740, and Edwards, along with others, began to itinerate and preach in churches beyond their own town. This is the background for Edwards's most famous sermon, "Sinners in the Hands of an Angry God," preached in Enfield, Connecticut, in July 1741. Over the course of the next several years, revival fire spread once again. In time this period came to be known as the (First) Great Awakening.

Edwards's role in this work of revival was powerfully established by his written work. *Some Thoughts Concerning the Present Revival of Religion in New England* celebrated the revivals of this era. *A Treatise on Religious Affections* became an enduring defense of the true nature of a work of the Spirit, especially in movements of revival. In this particular work he defends revival and explains what does and does not constitute a work of God's Spirit in renewing the heart. It still remains a major work of importance on spiritual discernment. After his death, *A History of the Work of Redemption* was published. It demonstrated how God used revival movements to expand the kingdom of Christ over the whole earth. *A Faithful Narrative of Surprising Conversions,* written shortly after the revival in the 1730s, is what the title reveals, a testimony of the "surprising" nature and fruit of multiplied conversions.

But what about this little book, commonly known as *An Humble Attempt,* which you now hold? Why is this particular work on revival so important? The answer is to be found in two places. First, we can see the importance of this book within the work itself. The content is rich, moving, and hopeful. Second, we can observe its importance in the impact that it has had upon subsequent generations of believers.

Published in 1747, the original title contained, incredibly, 145 words! Here is a shortened version of the original title:

> *An Humble Attempt to Promote Explicit Agreement and Visible Union of God's People in Extraordinary Prayer for the Revival of Religion and the Advancement of Christ's Kingdom on Earth, Pursuant to Scripture Promises and Prophecies Concerning the Last Time.*

In the aftermath of the Great Awakening there were many who felt the whole business amounted to very little when it was all over. Edwards disagreed. *An Humble Attempt* was published for this very reason. It is the fruit of many years of thought and study. As you will soon see, Edwards does more than merely defend revivals. He expounds the meaning of Zechariah 8:20–22 and urges prayer for new outpourings of the Spirit. But the prayer he urges is of a very specific sort—namely, *united* prayer that will demonstrate and reveal visible union among the churches. It is not just prayer that is needed, but "extraordinary prayer." And this prayer is not vague, for it must promote the "explicit agreement and visible union" of Christians. Literally, each word in this title bears upon the very nature of the "extraordinary" prayer that Edwards urges upon the reader.

In 1745 Edwards wrote a friend saying, "In many places where God of late wonderfully appeared he has now in a great measure withdrawn; and the consequence is, that Zion and the interest of religion are involved in innumerable and inextricable difficulties." During the later years of Edwards's life the situation changed very little. The tides of revival were out! Only God could bring the blessings the church needed.

So why did Edwards write this little treatise? I think there are at least two obvious reasons. First, he was a biblical optimist regarding the work of God. He sincerely believed that greater things and better times must come. He based this belief upon a multitude of texts that speak of a greater work of the Spirit bringing glory to Christ throughout the earth in the last days. He would have found nothing in the present doomsday eschatology of many modern evangelicals to fuel passion and hope for revival. His confidence was not vague; it was focused. He believed that Christ would save a multitude of people *and* claim the world for himself before the final judgment. (Though Edwards clearly was postmillennial in his view of Revelation 20, one does not have to share this system of doctrine to embrace his optimism!) He wrote to a friend in 1744, before this work was published, saying "that God will revive his work, and that what has been so great and very extraordinary, is a forerunner of a yet more glorious and extensive work."

Second, Edwards believed that the revival he had seen in his congregation in 1734–1735, and again in the wider New England context in the early 1740s, was a distinct and gracious work of God. The fact that the tides were now out did not negate that they had once washed ashore with great power, changing lives and refreshing the church. He wanted to conserve the good of this movement and foster greater demonstrations of divine blessing in coming centuries. Believing that God alone would send such times of refreshing, Edwards wanted to connect the promises of Scripture to the place of "extraordinary" prayer for revival for generations to come.

The *Humble Attempt* arose from a very practical source. It was Jonathan Edwards's response to a "Memorial" published by a group of Scottish ministers who had been involved in prayer societies, especially among young people, that began in Scotland around 1740. A group of godly ministers felt it was time to take this movement of prayer to a deeper level of resolve and practice. They created an "experiment" that would unite the prayer groups in Scotland into a unified, visible strategy. They specifically appealed to Christians to gather for revival, praying every Saturday evening and Sunday morning for the next two years! In addition, they urged special meetings on the first Tuesday of each quarter. They set the time of two years to see what God would do and then to proceed based upon the direction they believed the Lord gave them. In 1746, when they considered what had been accomplished in this two-year period, they believed they should issue an appeal to the church worldwide, especially in the American colonies. This led to the publication of the *Memorial.* Five hundred copies were sent to Boston. One of these came into Edwards's possession, and the result was *An Humble Attempt.*

David Bryant has suggested, correctly I think, that Edwards was prompted to write this treatise because of "its potential for mobilization, and its inherent value for holding Christians accountable to the work of prayer." (This is a correct reading of what you will see in the opening few pages of the book.) But there was more. Edwards, always rightly concerned that piety and prayer be rooted in sound theology, wanted to provide further theological support for this "extraordinary" revival prayer movement.

Edwards regarded the idea of Christians united in prayer as "exceeding beautiful, and becoming Christians" and most fitting given the present state of weakness and division. He added that "it is apparent that we can't help ourselves, and have nowhere else to go, but to God." But over the course of the next few years (1744–1745) Edwards could have been easily discouraged and given up such prayer. He wrote in May 1745, in a private letter, that the concert of prayer in Northampton had been anything but a great success.

Believing that the God who has determined the end of all things must be sought on the basis of his promises of mercy, Edwards continued to work for union among believers, for he saw union as a solution to New England's religious apathy. Christians praying together might eventually constitute "one family, one holy and happy society." And he reasoned, "Who knows what it may come to at last?" Perhaps these concerts would be used to "open the doors and windows of heaven that have so long been shut up, and been as brass over the heads of the inhabitants of the earth, to spiritual showers." Less than a year after Edwards expressed these sentiments he wrote *An Humble Attempt.*

The content of Edwards's argument follows three parts. After looking at the *Memorial* of the Scottish ministers he presents his case for prayer from Zechariah 8. He demonstrates that the prophecy of Zechariah addressed a last great time of prosperity for the church. He reasons that nothing in the early ages of the church fulfilled these promises. In a masterful way he argues that earlier periods of spiritual prosperity and blessing were types or anticipations (or down payments if you please) of the last and final age. Ministers in the Puritan tradition believed that God was sometimes pictured in Scripture as "hiding himself from the church." What are the people of God to do in such times? They answered that Christians should unite themselves with other earnest believers and seek the Lord in a constant and fervent way for showers of blessing. This is what Jonathan Edwards hoped to do by opening up this text for his readers. Finally, Edwards presents the reader with motives for united prayer and then seeks to answer objections to such a united movement.

I noted earlier that there are two reasons for the importance of this book. One is to be found in the content, as I briefly noted. The other reason is to be seen in the impact that this small book has had upon Christians for more than 250 years. In the view of Jonathan Edwards the Bible is a book filled with "precepts, encouragements, and examples" all underscoring the church's continual prayer for the gift of the Holy Spirit. This, I believe, is what makes this book so important today.

Jesus, teaching his disciples how to pray, said:

> Which of you fathers, if your son asks for a fish, will give him a snake instead? Or if he asks for an egg, will give him a scorpion? If you then, though you are evil, know how to give good gifts to your children, how much more will your Father in heaven give the Holy Spirit to those who ask him? (Luke 11:11–13 NIV)

I meet few Christians in the West who earnestly and faithfully ask the Father to "give the Holy Spirit" to the church. We assume that all that we should have, indeed all that we should expect, has already been given. Our prayers are small, and our passion is thus cooled. The breezes of modernism blow through evangelical congregations as well as liberal ones. We do not believe that Pentecost was a specimen day, the beginning of a new age. Pentecostal believers often assume that they have all that God will do in this age if certain gifts have been granted to them. Non-Pentecostal believers are content with a clear evidence of faith in Christ and often settle for a passionless, arid spirituality. Edwards stands against these two paradigms. For this reason his work is not denominationally sectarian but truly catholic. It is not accidental, to my mind, that worldwide movements of prayer for awakening have been birthed and nurtured by this marvelous book. My prayer is that a whole new movement of God's people will grow in "explicit agreement" and "extraordinary prayer, for the revival of religion and the advancement of Christ's kingdom on earth" according to the biblical promises that warrant such an effort. Even if we do not see the greatest outpouring of God's Spirit in history during our time, we are, by such ministries, putting "incense" into the golden bowls that are before the Lamb in heaven (Rev. 5:9). It is God's to grant the mercies and ours to ask. "Is anything too hard for the LORD?" (Gen. 18:14 NIV).

John H. Armstrong, president
Reformation and Revival Ministries

❧ *Part 1* ❧

THE PROPOSAL TO PRAY

ZECHARIAH 8:20–22

Thus saith the LORD of hosts, It shall yet come to pass, that there shall come people, and the inhabitants of many cities, and the inhabitants of one city shall go to another, saying, Let us go speedily to pray before the LORD, and to seek the LORD of hosts: I will go also. Yea, many people and strong nations shall come to seek the LORD of hosts in Jerusalem, and to pray before the LORD.

❖ Chapter 1 ❖

A VISION FOR THE LATTER DAYS

In these introductory remarks Edwards summarizes his sense of what God intends for his church in the latter days, showing from many parts of Scripture that God is planning to bring great revival and growth to his church, subsequent to a season of united and earnest prayer on the part of his people.

❖

EXPLANATORY INTRODUCTION: A PROPHECY FOR THE LATTER DAYS

In this chapter we have a prophecy of a future glorious advancement of the church of God; wherein it is evident that something further is intended than ever was fulfilled to the *Jewish* nation under the Old Testament. For here are plain prophecies of such things as never were fulfilled before the coming of the *Messiah:* particularly, what is said in the two last verses in the chapter, of *many people and strong nations worshiping and seeking the true God;* and of so great an accession of *Gentile* nations to the church of God that by far the greater part of the visible worshipers should consist of this new accession, so that they should be to the other as *ten to one*—certain number for an uncertain. There never happened anything, from the time of the prophet *Zechariah* to the coming of Christ, to answer this prophecy: and it can have no fulfillment but either, in the calling of the *Gentiles,* in and after the days of the *apostles;* or, in the future glorious enlargement of the church of God in the *latter ages* of the world, so often foretold by the prophets of the Old Testament, and by the prophet *Zechariah* in particular, in the latter part of his prophecy. It is most probably that what the Spirit of God has chiefly respect to is that *last* and greatest enlargement and most glorious advancement of the church of God on earth; in the benefits of which especially the *Jewish* nation were to have a share, a very eminent and distinguished share.

There is great agreement between what is here said and other prophecies that *must* manifestly have respect to the church's latter-day glory: "The Lord shall arise upon thee, and his glory shall be seen upon thee: and the Gentiles shall come to thy light, and kings to the brightness of thy rising. Lift up thine eyes round about, and see; all they gather themselves together, they come to thee" (Isa. 60:2–4). That whole chapter, beyond all dispute, has respect to the most glorious state of the church of God on earth. "Shall the earth be made to bring forth in one day? Shall a nation be born at once?" (Isa. 66:8). "Rejoice ye with *Jerusalem,* and be glad with her, all ye that love her"

(Isa. 66:10). "I will extend peace to her like a river, and the glory of the Gentiles like a flowing stream" (Isa. 66:12). "But in the last day it shall come to pass that the mountain of the house of the Lord shall be established in the top of the mountains, and it shall be exalted above the hills, and people shall flow unto it; and many nations shall come, and say, Come, and let us go up to the mountain of the Lord, and to the house of the God of *Jacob*. And he shall judge among many people, and rebuke strong nations afar off; and they shall beat their swords into plowshares, and their spears into pruning-hooks; nation shall not lift up sword against nation, neither shall they learn war any more" (Mic. 4:1–3). So also Isaiah 2 at the beginning. There has been nothing yet brought to pass, in any measure, to answer these prophecies. And as the prophecy in my text, and the following verse, agrees with them, so there is reason to think it has a respect to the same times. And indeed there is a remarkable agreement in the description given throughout the chapter, with the representations made of those times elsewhere in the prophets.

So that however the prophet, in some parts of this chapter, may have respect to future smiles of heaven on the *Jewish* nation, lately returned from the *Babylonish* captivity, and resettled in the land of *Canaan,* in a great increase of their numbers and wealth, and the return of more captives from *Chaldea* and other countries, yet the Spirit of God has doubtless respect to things far *greater* than these, and of which these were but faint resemblances. We find it common in the prophecies of the Old Testament that when the prophets are speaking of divine favors and blessings on the *Jews,* attending or following their return from the *Babylonish* captivity, the Spirit of God takes occasion from thence to speak of the incomparably greater blessings on the church that shall attend and follow her deliverance from the spiritual or mystical *Babylon,* of which those were a type; and then speaks almost wholly of these latter and vastly greater things, so as to seem to forget the former.

And whereas the prophet, in this chapter, speaks of God *bringing his people again from the east and west to* Jerusalem (Zech. 8:7–8) *and multitudes of all nations taking hold of the skirts of the* Jews; so far as this means literally the nation of the posterity of Jacob, it cannot chiefly respect any return of the Jews from Babylon and other countries, in those ancient times before Christ; for no such things attended any such return. It must therefore have respect to the great calling and gathering of the Jews into the fold of *Christ,* and their being received to the blessings of his kingdom, after the fall of *antichrist,* or the destruction of his mystical Babylon.

Observations on the Text

In the text we have an account *how* this future glorious advancement of the church of God should be introduced, namely, by great multitudes in different towns and countries taking up a *joint resolution,* and coming into an express and *visible agreement* that they will, by united and extraordinary *prayer,* seek to God that he would come and manifest himself, and grant the tokens and fruits of his gracious presence. Particularly we may observe:

The duty of prayer

The *duty,* with the attendance on which the glorious event foretold shall be brought on, is the duty of *prayer.* Prayer, some suppose, is here to be taken *synechdochically*[1] for the whole of divine *worship,* prayer being a *principal part* of worship in the days of the gospel, when sacrifices are abolished. If so, this is to be understood only as a prophecy of a great *revival* of religion, and of the true worship of God among his visible people, the *accession* of others to the church, and turning of multitudes from idolatry to the worship of the true God. But it appears to me reasonable to suppose that something more *special* is intended, with regard to the duty of prayer; considering that prayer is here expressly and repeatedly mentioned; and also considering how parallel this place is with many other prophecies that speak of an *extraordinary* spirit of prayer, as preceding and introducing that glorious day of religious revival, and advancement of the church's peace and prosperity, so often foretold. Add to this, the agreeableness of what is here said, with what is said afterwards by the same prophet, of the *pouring out of a spirit of grace and supplication,* as that with which this great revival of religion shall begin (cf. Zech. 12:10).

1. That is, as a symbolic element representing the whole—worship—of which it—prayer—is a part.

The good to be sought in prayer

The *good* that shall be sought by prayer is God himself. It is said once and again, "They shall go to pray before the Lord, and to seek the Lord of hosts." This is the *good* they ask for, and seek by prayer, *the Lord of hosts* himself. To *seek God,* as the expression may perhaps be sometimes used in Scripture, may signify no more than seeking the *favor* or *mercy* of God. And if it be taken so here, *praying before the Lord,* and *seeking the Lord of hosts,* must be synonymous expressions. And it must be confessed to be a common thing in Scripture to signify the same thing repeatedly, by various expressions of the same import, for the greater emphasis.

But certainly the expression of *seeking the Lord* is very commonly used to signify something more; it implies that *God himself* is the great *good* desired and sought after; that the blessings pursued are God's gracious presence, the blessed manifestations of him, union and intercourse with him; or, in short, God's *manifestation* and *communications* of himself by his Holy Spirit. Thus the psalmist *desired God, thirsted after him,* and *sought him* (Ps. 42:2). "O God, thou art my God; early will I *seek thee.* My flesh longeth for *thee,* in a dry and thirsty land, where no water is; to see thy power and thy glory, so as I have seen thee in the sanctuary. My soul followeth hard after thee" (Ps. 63:1–2, 8). "Whom have I in heaven but thee? And there is none upon earth that I desire besides thee" (Ps. 73:25). The psalmist earnestly pursued after GOD, *his soul thirsted after him, he stretched forth his hands unto him,* and so forth (Ps. 143:6). And therefore it is in Scripture the peculiar character of the saints, that they are *those who seek* GOD: "This is the generation of them that seek *him*" (Ps. 24:6). "Your heart shall live that seek *God*" (Ps. 69:32). If the expression in the text [Zech. 8:20–22] be understood agreeably to this sense, then by *seeking the Lord of hosts,* we must understand a seeking that God who had withdrawn, or as it were hid himself for a long time, would return to his church, and grant the tokens and fruits of his gracious presence, and those blessed communications of his Spirit to his people, and to mankind on earth, which he had often promised, and which his church had long waited for.

And it seems reasonable to understand the phrase, *seeking the Lord of hosts,* in this sense here; and not as *merely* signifying the same thing as *praying* to God: not only because the expression is repeatedly *added* to *praying before the Lord* in the text; but also because the phrase, taken in this sense, is exactly agreeable to other parallel prophetic representations. Thus God's people seeking, by earnest prayer, the promised restoration of the church of God, after the *Babylonish* captivity, and the great apostasy that occasioned it, is called their SEEKING GOD, and SEARCHING *for him;* and God's granting this promised revival and restoration is called his being FOUND *of them.* "For thus saith the Lord, that after seventy years be accomplished at *Babylon,* I will visit you, and perform my good word towards you, in causing you to return to this place. For I know the thoughts that I think towards you, saith the Lord, thoughts of peace, and not of evil, to give you an expected end. Then shall ye go and call upon me, and I will hearken unto you; and ye shall *seek me* and *find me,* when ye shall *search for me* with all your heart; and I will be *found* of you, saith the Lord, and I will turn away your captivity" (Jer. 29:10–14). And the prophets, from time to time, represent God, in a low and afflicted state of his church, as being *withdrawn,* and *hiding himself.* "Verily thou art a God that hidest thyself, O God of Israel, the Savior" (Isa. 45:15). "I hid me, and was wroth" (Isa. 57:17). And they represent God's people, while his church is in such a state, before God delivers and restores the same, as *seeking him, looking for him, searching and waiting for him,* and *calling after him.* "I will go and return unto my place, till they acknowledge their offense, and seek my face from the house of *Jacob,* and I will look for him" (Hos. 5:15).

And when God, in answer to their prayers and succeeding their endeavors, delivers, restores, and advances his church, according to his promise, then he is said to *answer,* and *come,* and *say, Here am I,* and to *show himself;* and they are said to *find him,* and *see him plainly.* "Then shalt thou *cry,* and ye shall say, *Here I am*" (Isa. 58:9). "I said not unto the seed of Jacob, *Seek ye me* in vain" (Isa. 45:19). "The Lord will wipe away the tears from off all faces, and the rebuke of his people shall he take away from off the earth. And it shall be said in that day, Lo, this is our God, we have *waited for him,* and he will save us: This is the Lord, we have *waited* for *him;* we will be glad and rejoice in his salvation" (Isa. 25:8–9); together with the next chapter (Isa. 26:8–9), we have waited for thee; "the desire of our soul is to thy name, and to the remembrance of thee. With my soul have I desired thee in the night; yea, with my spirit within me will I *seek thee* early. For when thy judgments are in the earth, the inhabitants of the world will learn righteousness." "Therefore my people shall know my name; therefore they shall know in that day, that I am he that doth speak: *behold, it is I.* How beautiful upon the mountains are the feet of him that bringeth good tidings, that publisheth peace, that bringeth good tidings of good, that publisheth salvation, that saith unto Zion, Thy God reigneth! Thy watchmen shall lift up the voice, together they shall sing; for they shall see eye to eye, when the Lord shall bring again Zion" (Isa. 52:6–8).

Who are to be united in seeking the Lord

We may observe *who* they are that shall be *united* in thus seeking the Lord of hosts: *the inhabitants of many cities,* and of many countries, *yea, many people, and strong nations,* great multitudes in different parts of the world shall conspire in this business. From the representation made in the prophecy, it appears rational to suppose that it will be fulfilled something after this manner: There shall be given much of a spirit of prayer to God's people, in many places, disposing them to come into an express *agreement,* unitedly to pray to God in an extraordinary manner that he would appear for the help of his church, and in mercy to mankind, and *pour out his Spirit, revive his work,* and advance his spiritual *kingdom* in the world, as he has promised. This disposition to prayer, and union in it, will gradually spread more and more, and increase to greater degrees; with which at length will gradually be introduced a *revival of religion,* and a disposition to greater engagedness in the worship and service of God, amongst his professing people. This being observed, will be the means of awakening others, making them sensible of the wants of their souls, and exciting in them a great concern for their spiritual and everlasting good, and putting them upon earnestly crying to God for spiritual mercies, and disposing them to join in that extraordinary seeking and serving of God.

In this manner *religion* shall be *propagated,* till the awakening reaches those that are in the *highest stations,* and till *whole nations* be awakened, and there be at length an accession of many of the chief nations of the world to the church of God. Thus after the inhabitants of many cities of Israel, or of God's professing people, have taken up and pursued a joint resolution, to go and pray before the Lord, and seek the Lord of hosts, others shall be drawn to worship and serve him with them; till at length *many people and strong nations* shall join themselves to them; and there shall, in process of time, be a vast accession to the church, so that it shall be *ten* times as large as it was before; yea, at length, all nations shall be converted unto God. Thus "ten men shall take hold, out of all the languages of the nations, of the skirt of him that is a Jew" (in the sense of the apostle, Rom. 2:28–29) "saying, We will go with you; for we have heard, that God is with you" (Zech. 8:23). And thus shall be fulfilled Psalm 65:2, "O thou that hearest prayer, *unto thee shall all flesh come."*

The mode of their uniting together in prayer

We may observe the *mode* of their *union* in this duty. It is a *visible* union, an union by *explicit agreement,* a joint resolution declared by one to another, being first proposed by some, and readily and expressly followed by others. The inhabitants of *one city* shall apply themselves to the inhabitants of *another,* saying, *Let us go,* etc. Those to whom the motion is made, shall *comply* with it, the proposal shall take with *many,* it shall be a *prevailing, spreading* thing; one shall follow another's example, one and another *shall say, I will go also.* Some suppose that the words, *I will go also,* are to be taken as the words of him that makes the proposal; as much as to say, I do not propose *that* to you which I am not willing to do myself. I desire *you* to go, and am ready to go *with you.* But this is to suppose no more to be expressed in these latter words than was expressed before in the proposal itself; for these words, *let us go,* signify as much. It seems to me much more natural, to understand these latter words as importing the *consent* of those to whom the proposal is made, or the *reply* of one and another that falls in with it. This is much more agreeable to the plain design of the text, which is to represent the *concurrence* of great numbers in this affair; and more agreeable to the representation made in the next verse, of one following another, many *taking hold of the skirt of him that is a Jew.*

And though, if the words be thus understood, we must suppose an *ellipsis* in the text, something understood that is not expressed, as if it had been said, *those of other cities shall say,*

I will go also; yet, this is not difficult to be supposed, for such *ellipses* are very common in Scripture. We have one exactly parallel with it in Jeremiah 3:22: "Return, ye backsliding children, and I will heal your backslidings. Behold, we have come unto thee; for thou art the Lord our God," i.e., the backsliding children shall say, "Behold, we come unto thee," etc. And in Song of Songs 4:16 and 5:1, "Let my beloved come into his garden, and eat his pleasant fruits. I am come into my garden, my sister, my spouse," i.e., her beloved shall say, "I am come into my garden." We have the like throughout that song. So "the heavens shall declare his righteousness; for God is Judge himself. Hear, O my people, and I will speak" (Ps. 50:6–7), i.e., the Judge shall say, "Hear, O my people," etc. So Psalm 132:1–2: The psalms and prophets abound with such figures of speech.

The manner of prayer agreed on

We may observe the *manner of prayer* agreed on, or the manner in which they agree, to *engage in and perform the duty. Let us go SPEEDILY to pray;* or, as it is in the margin, Let us go *continually.* The words literally translated are, *Let us go in going.* Such an ingemination, or doubling of words, is very common in the Hebrew language, when it is intended that a thing shall be very *strongly* expressed. It generally implies the *superlative degree* of a thing; as the *holy of holies* signifies the most holy. But it commonly denotes, not only the utmost *degree* of a thing, but also the utmost *certainty;* as when God said to Abraham, "In multiplying, I will multiply thy seed" (Gen. 22:17), it implies both that God would *cer-*

tainly multiply his seed, and also multiply it *exceedingly.* So when God said to Adam, "In the day that thou eatest thereof, in dying thou shalt die" (as the words are in the original), it implies, both that he should *surely die,* and also that he should die most *terribly,* should utterly perish, and be destroyed to the utmost degree.

In short, as the ingemination of words in the Hebrew generally denotes the strength of expression, so it is used to signify almost all those things that are wont to be signified by the various forms of strong speech in other languages. It signifies not only the utmost *degree* of a thing, and great *certainty;* but also the *peremptoriness* and *terribleness* of a threatening, the *greatness* and *positiveness* of a promise, the *strictness* of a command, and the *earnestness* of a request. When God says to Adam, "Dying thou shalt die," it is equivalent to such strong expressions in English, as, *Thou shalt die surely, or indeed;* or, *Thou shalt die with a witness.* So when it is said in the text, "Let us go in going, and pray before the Lord," the strength of the expression represents the *earnestness* of those that make the proposal, their great *engagedness* in the affair. And with respect to the *duty* proposed, it may be understood to signify that they should be *speedy, fervent,* and *constant* in it; or, in one word, that it should be *thoroughly* performed.

Such prayer a happy thing

We may learn from the tenor of this prophecy, together with the context, that this union in such prayer is foretold as a *becoming* and *happy* thing, what would be acceptable to God, and attended with glorious success.

From the whole we may infer that it is a very *suitable* thing, and *well-pleasing to God,* for many people, in different parts of the world, by express *agreement,* to come into a *visible union* in extraordinary, speedy, fervent, and constant *prayer,* for those great effusions of the *Holy Spirit,* which shall bring on that *advancement* of Christ's church and kingdom that God has so often promised shall be in the *latter ages* of the world. And so from hence I would infer the *duty* of God's people, proposing a *method* for such an *union* as has been spoken of, in extraordinary prayer, for this great mercy.[2]

STUDY QUESTIONS

1. Peter announced that the "latter days" so often referred to in prophetic literature began with the pouring out of God's Spirit on the first Pentecost (see Acts 2:14–17). From what you know about the Book of Acts, how can you see that what was prophesied in Zechariah 8:20–22 began to be realized in the period of the early church?

2. In order not to clutter this study of prayer and revival with unnecessary or perhaps even distracting historical details, we have omitted all reference to the *Memorial* Edwards had received from Scotland concerning prayer for revival, as well as the historical circumstances leading up to that. This part of *An Humble Attempt* is found in part I, sections 3 and 4 of the Hickman edition, vol. I, of the *Works* of Jonathan Edwards.

2. Summarize Edwards's vision for what we should expect to see in the "latter days." Do you see any evidence that this is presently occurring?

3. Reflect on the church's role in culture, society, and moral issues over the past couple of generations. Does anything about the current situation of the church in our world suggest, appearances to the contrary notwithstanding (new churches, megachurches, a thriving evangelical subculture, etc.), that God may have withdrawn himself or may be in hiding from his church at this time? In what ways can you see that the church might be ripe for a new season of revival?

4. Edwards's point, following Zechariah, is that seasons of revival follow seasons of prayer on the part of God's people. How would you describe the kind of prayer Edwards has in mind? What would that look like in your life? In your church? In the church in America, or in the world?

5. Set some goals for this study of Edwards on prayer and revival. What do you hope to learn? How do you hope to see your work of prayer affected? What would you like to see happen in your church? Among the churches in your community? What would that require of you?

❈ *Part 2* ❈

MOTIVES FOR SUCH PRAYER

❊ Chapter 2 ❊

A GREAT ADVANCEMENT REMAINS

In this section Edwards puts forth his argument that the time of Christ's reigning over and ruling the whole earth, and of the flourishing of the church and true religion, is yet to come, and shall come on this earth in this historical time period, before the end of all things. And the hope of this, Edwards wants to insist, should be great incentive for the saints of God to unite in prayer that God might do it.

❊

I proceed to the second thing intended in this Discourse, namely, to offer to consideration some things, which may tend to induce the people of God to comply with the proposal and request [that they should unite in prayer for revival].

THE WITNESS OF THE OLD TESTAMENT

It is evident from Scripture that there is *yet remaining* a great *advancement* of the interest of *religion* and the *king-*

dom of Christ in this world, by an *abundant outpouring of the Spirit of God,* far greater and more extensive than ever yet has been. It is certain that many things, which are spoken concerning a *glorious* time of the church's *enlargement* and *prosperity* in the *latter days,* have never yet been fulfilled. There has never yet been any propagation and prevalence of religion, in any wise, of that *extent* and *universality* which the prophecies represent. It is often foretold and signified, in a great variety of strong expressions, that there should a time come, when *all nations,* throughout the whole habitable world, should embrace the true religion, and be brought into the church of God. It was often promised to the patriarchs that "in their seed all the nations, or (as it is sometimes expressed) all the families of the earth shall be blessed." Agreeably to this, it is said of the Messiah "that all nations shall serve him" (Ps. 72:11); and "Men shall be blessed in him, and all nations shall call him blessed" (Ps. 72:17). And in Isaiah 2:2 it is said that "all nations shall flow unto the mountain of the house of the Lord." And "that all nations shall be gathered unto the name of the Lord to Jerusalem, and shall walk no more after the imagination of their evil heart" (Jer. 3:17). "That all flesh shall come and worship before the Lord" (Isa. 66:23). "And that all flesh should see the glory of God together" (Isa. 60:5). "And that all flesh should come to him that hears prayer" (Ps. 65:2). Christ compares the *kingdom of heaven* in this world "to leaven, which a woman took and hid in three measures of meal, till the whole was leavened" (Matt. 13:33).

The whole world to be given to Christ

It is natural and reasonable to suppose that the whole world should finally be given to Christ, as one whose right it is to reign, as the proper heir of him who is originally the King of all nations, and the possessor of heaven and earth. And the Scripture teaches us that God the Father hath constituted his Son, as God-man, in his kingdom of grace, or mediatorial kingdom, to be the *heir of the world,* that he might in this kingdom have "the heathen for his inheritance, and the utmost ends of the earth for his possession" (Heb. 1:2; 2:8; Ps. 2:6–8). Thus Abraham is said to be *the heir of the world,* not in himself, but in *his seed,* which is Christ (Rom. 4:13). And how was this to be fulfilled to Abraham, but by God's fulfilling that great promise that "in his seed all the nations of the earth should be blessed"? For that promise is what the apostle is speaking of: which shows that God has appointed Christ to be the heir of the world in his kingdom of grace, and to possess and reign over all nations, through the propagation of his gospel, and the power of his Spirit communicating the blessings of it. God hath appointed him to this universal dominion by a solemn oath: "I have sworn by myself, the word is gone out of my mouth in righteousness, and shall not return, that unto me every knee shall bow, and every tongue shall swear" (Isa. 45:23; cf. Phil. 2:10–11). Though the solemn oath of God the Father is to be understood in so comprehensive a sense as to extend to what shall be accomplished at the day of judgment, yet it is evident by the foregoing and following verses that the thing most directly intended is what shall be fulfilled by the spreading of the gospel of his salvation, and the power of the Spirit of grace, bringing "all the ends of the earth to look to him that they may be saved," and come to him for "righteousness and strength, that in him they might be justified, and might glory."

His kingdom of far greater extent

God has suffered many earthly princes to extend their conquests over a great part of the face of the earth, and to possess a dominion of vast extent, and one monarchy to conquer and succeed another, the latter being still the greater; it is reasonable to suppose that a much greater glory in this respect should be reserved for Christ, God's own Son and rightful heir, who has purchased the dominion by so great and hard a service: it is reasonable to suppose that his dominion should be far the largest, and his conquests vastly the greatest and most extensive. And thus the Scriptures represent the matter, in Nebuchadnezzar's vision, and the prophet's interpretation (Dan. 2). There four great monarchies of the earth, one succeeding another, are represented by the great image of gold, silver, brass, iron, and clay; but at last a stone, cut out of the mountain without hands, smites the image upon his feet, which breaks the iron, clay, brass, silver, and gold in pieces that all become as the chaff of the summer threshing floors, and the wind carries them away, that no place is found for them; but the stone waxes great, becomes a great mountain, and *fills the whole earth:* signifying the kingdom which the Lord God of heaven should set up in the world, last of all, which should break in pieces and consume all other kingdoms. Surely this representation leads us to suppose that this last kingdom shall be of much greater extent than any of the preceding.

The like representation is made in the seventh chapter of Daniel; there the four monarchies are represented by four great beasts that arose successively, on conquering and subduing another; the fourth and last of these is said to be dreadful and terrible, and strong exceedingly, and to have great iron teeth, and to devour and break in pieces, and stamp the residue with his feet; yea, it is said that the kingdom represented by this beast shall devour the whole earth: but last of all, one like the Son of man appears, coming to the Ancient of days, and being brought near before him, receiving of him a dominion and glory, and a kingdom *that all people, nations, and languages* should serve him (Dan. 7:23). This last circumstance, of the vast extent and universality of his dominion, is manifestly spoken of as one thing greatly distinguishing this holy kingdom from all the preceding monarchies. Although of one of the former it was said that it should *devour the whole earth,* yet we are naturally led, both by the much greater emphasis and strength of the expressions, as well as by the whole connection and tenor of the prophecy, to understand the universality here expressed in a much more extensive and absolute sense. And the terms used in the interpretation of this vision are such that scarcely any can be devised more strong, to signify an absolute universality of dominion over the inhabitants of the face of the earth (Dan. 7:27). "And the kingdom and the dominion, and the greatness of the kingdom under the whole heaven, shall be given to the people of the most high God." Agreeably to this, the gospel is represented as "preached unto them that dwell on the earth, and to every nation, and tongue, and kindred, and people" (Rev. 14:6).

The universal prevalence of true religion in the latter days is sometimes expressed by its reaching to the "utmost ends of the earth" (Ps. 2:8); "to all the ends of the earth, and of the world" (Pss. 22:27; 67:7; 98:3; Isa. 45:22); "all the ends of the earth, with those that are far off upon the sea" (Ps. 65:5); "from the rising of the sun to the going down of the same" (Ps. 113:3; Mal. 1:11); "the outgoing of the morning and of the evening" (Ps. 65:8). It seems that all the most strong expressions that were in use among the *Jews* to signify the habitable world in its utmost extent are used to signify the extent of the church of God in the latter days. And in many places, a *variety* of these expressions is used, and there is an accumulation of them, expressed with great force.

The knowledge of God over the whole earth

It would be unreasonable to say, these are only bold *figures,* used after the manner of the *eastern* nations, to express the great extent of the Christian church, at and after the days of *Constantine.* To say so, would be in effect to say that it would have been impossible for God, if he had desired it, plainly to have foretold anything that should absolutely have extended to all nations of the earth. I question whether it be possible to find out a more strong expression, to signify an absolute universality of the knowledge of the true religion through the habitable world, than that in Isaiah 11:9: "The earth shall be full of the knowledge of the Lord, *as the waters cover the sea.*" Which is as much as to say, as there is no place in the vast ocean where there is not water, so there shall be no part of the world of mankind where there is not the knowledge of the Lord; as there is no part of the wide bed or cavity possessed by the sea, but what is covered with water, so there shall be no part of the habitable world that shall not be covered by the light of the gospel, and possessed by the true religion. *Waters* are often in prophecy put for nations and multitudes of people. So the waters of the main ocean seem sometimes to be put for the inhabitants of the earth in general, as in Ezekiel's vision of the waters of the sanctuary, and ran east, till they came to the ocean, and were at first a small stream, but continually increased till they became a great river; and when they came to the sea, the water even of the vast ocean was *healed* (Ezek. 47:8), representing the conversion of the world to the true religion in the latter days.

False religions and unbelieving nations abolished

It seems evident that the time will come, when there will not be one nation remaining in the world, which shall not embrace the true religion, in that God has expressly revealed that no one such nation shall be left standing on the earth: "The nation and kingdom that will not serve thee shall perish; yea, those nations shall be utterly wasted" (Isa. 60:12). "God has declared that heathen idolatry and all the worship of false gods shall be wholly abolished, in the most universal manner, so that it shall be continued in no place under the heavens, or upon the face of the earth: "The gods that have not made the heavens and the earth, even they shall perish from the earth, and from under these heavens" (Jer. 10:11). "They are vanity, and the work of errors, in the time of their visitation they shall perish" (Jer. 10:15). This must be understood as what shall be brought to pass while *this earth* and these *heavens* remain, i.e., before the end of the world. Agreeable to this is Isaiah 54:1–2, "Sing, O barren, thou that didst not bear; for more are the children of the desolate than the children of the married wife, saith the Lord. Enlarge the place of thy tent, and let them stretch forth the curtains of thy habitation: spare not, lengthen thy cords, strengthen thy stakes." "For thy Maker is thy husband; the Lord of Hosts is his name; and thy Redeemer the Holy One of Israel; *The God of the whole earth shall he be called*" (Isa. 54:5).

THE WITNESS OF
THE NEW TESTAMENT

The prophecies of the *New Testament* do no less evidently show that a time will come when the gospel shall universally prevail, and the kingdom of Christ be extended over the whole habitable earth, in the most proper sense.

The universal dominion of Christ

Christ says, "I, if I be lifted up from the earth, will draw all men unto me" (John 12:32). It is fit, that when the Son of God becomes man, he should have dominion over all mankind. It is fit that since he became an inhabitant of the earth, and shed his blood on the earth, he should possess the whole earth. It is fit, seeing here he became a servant, and was subject to men, and was arraigned before them, and judged, condemned, and executed by them, and suffered ignominy and death in a most public manner, before *Jews* and *Gentiles*—being *lifted up* to view on the cross upon a hill, near that populous city *Jerusalem,* at a most public time, when there were many hundred thousand spectators, from all parts—that [he] should be rewarded with an universal dominion over mankind; and it is here declared he shall be.

The witness of Paul

The apostle, in the eleventh [chapter] of Romans, teaches us to look on that great outpouring of the Spirit, and ingathering of souls into Christ's kingdom, in those days, first of the *Jews* and then of the *Gentiles,* to be but as the *first-fruits* of the intended harvest, both with regard to *Jews* and *Gentiles,* as a sign that all should in due time be gathered in: "For if the *first-fruit* be holy, *the lump* is also holy; and if the root be holy, so are the branches" (Rom. 11:16). And in that context, the apostle speaks of the FULLNESS of both *Jews* and *Gentiles,* as what shall hereafter be brought in, distinctly from the ingathering from among both, in those primitive ages of Christianity. In verse 12 we read of the *fullness of the Jews,* and in the twenty-fifth verse, of the *fullness of the Gentiles.* And in verses 30–32, the apostle teaches us to look upon that infidelity and darkness which first prevailed over all the Gentile nations, before Christ came, and *afterwards* over the *Jews,* as what was wisely permitted for the manifestation of the glory of God's mercy, in due time, on the whole world, constituted of *Jews* and *Gentiles.* "God hath concluded them all in unbelief, that he might have mercy upon all." These things plainly show that the time is coming when the *whole world* of mankind shall be brought into the church of Christ; the *fullness* of both, *the whole lump,* all the nation of the *Jews,* and all the world of the *Gentiles.*

The witness of Revelation

In the last great conflict between the church of Christ and her enemies, before the commencement of the glorious time of the church's peace and rest, *the kings of the earth and the* WHOLE WORLD are represented as *gathered together* (Rev. 16:14). And then *the seventh angel pours out his vial into the air,* which limits the kingdom of Satan, as god of this world; and that kingdom is represented as utterly overthrown (v. 17, etc.). In another description of that great battle (Rev. 19) Christ is represented as riding forth, having on his head *many crowns,* and on his vesture and on his thigh a name written, KING OF KINGS AND LORD OF LORDS. Which we may well suppose signifies that he is now going to that conquest, whereby he shall set up a kingdom, in which he shall be *King of kings,* in a far more extensive manner than either *Babylonish, Persian, Grecian,* or *Roman* monarchs were. And in verse 17, and following, *an angel* appears *standing in the sun* that overlooks the whole world, calling on "all the fowls that fly in the midst of heaven, to come and eat the flesh of kings." And in consequence of the great victory Christ gains at that time, "an angel comes down from heaven, having the key of the bottomless pit, and a great chain in his hand, and lays hold on the devil, and binds him, and casts him into the bottomless pit, and shuts him up, and sets a seal upon him, that he should deceive the nations no more." Satan being dispossessed of that highest monarchy on earth, the *Roman empire,* and cast out in the time of *Constantine* is represented (Rev. 12) by his being *cast down from heaven to the earth,* but now there is something far beyond that; he is cast *out of the earth,* and is shut up in *hell,* and confined to that place alone, so that he has no place left him in this world of mankind, high or low.

Now will any be so unreasonable as to say that all these things do not signify more than that one *third* part of the world should be brought into the church of Christ; beyond which it cannot be pretended that the Christian religion has ever yet reached, in its greatest extent? Those countries which belonged to the *Roman* empire, that were brought to the profession of Christianity after the reign of *Constantine,* are but a small part of what the habitable world now is. As to extent of ground, they altogether bear, I suppose, no greater proportion to it than the land of *Canaan* did to the *Roman* empire. And our Redeemer in his kingdom of grace has hitherto possessed but a little part of the world, in its most flourishing state, since arts are arisen to their greatest height; and a very great part of the world is but lately discovered, and much remains undiscovered to this day. These things make it very evident that the *main fulfillment* of those prophecies that speak of the glorious advancement of Christ's kingdom on *earth* is still to come.

Universality and Great Duration

And as there has been nothing as yet, with regard to the flourishing of religion, and the advancement of Christ's kingdom, of such *extent* as to answer the prophecies, so neither has there been anything of that *duration* that is foretold. The prophecies speak of *Jerusalem* being made *the joy of the whole earth,* and also the *joy of many generations* (Ps. 48:2; Isa. 60:15); that "God's people should long enjoy the work of their hands" (Isa. 65:22); that they should "reign with Christ a thousand years" (Rev. 20), by which we must at least understand a very long time. But it would be endless to mention all the places which signify that the time of the church's great peace and prosperity should be of long continuance. Almost all the prophecies that speak of her latter-day glory, imply it; and it is implied in very many of them that when once this day of the church's advancement and peace is begun, it shall never end till the world ends;

or, at least, that there shall be no more a return of her troubles and adversity for any considerable continuance. Then "the days of her mourning shall be ended"; her tribulations "be as the waters of *Noah* unto God, that as he has sworn that the waters of *Noah* should no more pass over the earth, so he will swear that he will no more be wroth with his people, or rebuke them."

It is implied that "God's people should no more walk after the imagination of their evil hearts; *that* God would hide himself no more from the house of *Israel*; because he has poured out his Spirit upon them; *that* their sun should no more go down, nor the moon withdraw itself; *that* the light should not be clear and dark" (i.e., there should be no more an interchange of light and darkness, as used to be), but that it *should be* all *one* continued *day; not day and night* (for so the words are in the original in Zech. 14:7), alternately, "but it shall come to pass, that at evening time (i.e., at the time that night and darkness used to be) it shall be light; *and that* the nations should beat their swords into plowshares, and their spears into pruning-hooks, and that nation should not lift up sword against nation, nor learn war any more; *but that* there should be an abundance of peace so long as the moon endureth."

So durable a state yet to be

But the church of Christ has never yet enjoyed a state of peace and prosperity for any *long* time; on the contrary, the time for her rest, and of the flourishing state of religion, have ever been very *short*. Hitherto the church may say, as in

Isaiah 63:17–18, "Return for thy servants' sake, the tribes of thine inheritance; the people of thy holiness have possessed it but a little while." The quietness that the church of God enjoyed at the beginning of *Constantine's* reign was very short. The peace the empire enjoyed, in freedom from war, was not more than twenty years; no longer nor greater than it had enjoyed under some of the heathen emperors. After this the empire was rent in pieces by intestine[1] wars, and wasted almost everywhere by the invasions and incursions of barbarous nations; and the Christian world, soon after, was all in contention and confusion, by heresies and divisions in matters of religion. And the church of Christ has never as yet been, for any long time, free from persecution; especially when truth has prevailed, and true religion flourished. It is manifest that hitherto the people of God have been kept under, and *Zion* has been in a low afflicted state, and her enemies have had the chief sway.

Another thing which makes it exceedingly manifest that the day of the church's greatest advancement on earth, which is foretold in Scripture, has never yet come, is that it is so plainly and expressly revealed, this day shall succeed the *last* of the four monarchies, even the *Roman,* in its *last* state, wherein it is divided into *ten kingdoms,* and after the destruction of the *antichrist,* signified by the *little horn,* whose reign is contemporary with the reign of the ten kings. These things are very plain in the second and seventh chapters of *Daniel,* and also in the *Revelation of St. John.* And it is also plain by the

1. That is, internal.

ninth chapter of *Romans,* that it shall be after the national conversion of the *Jews, which shall be as life from the dead to the Gentiles,* and *the fullness of both Jews and Gentiles shall be come in,* all the nations of the *Jews,* and all other nations, shall *obtain mercy,* and there shall be that general ingathering of the *harvest* of the whole earth, of which all that had been converted before, either of *Jews* or *Gentiles,* were but the *first-fruits.*

The last kingdom yet to come

Thus it is meet that the *last kingdom* which shall take place on *earth,* should be the kingdom of God's own *Son* and *heir,* whose right it is to rule and reign; and that whatever revolutions and confusions there may be in the world, for a long time, the cause of truth, the righteous cause, shall finally prevail, and God's holy people should at last *inherit the earth,* and *reign on earth;* and that the world should continue in tumults and great revolutions, following one another, from age to age, the world being as it were in *travail,* till truth and holiness are brought forth. It is meet that all things should be *shaken;* and that the wisdom of the Ruler of the world should be manifested in bringing all things ultimately to so good an issue. The world is made for the Son of God; his kingdom is the *end* of all changes that come to pass in the state of the world. All are only to prepare the way for this; it is fit, therefore, that the last kingdom on earth should be his. It is wisely and mercifully ordered of God that it should be so, on this account, as well as many others, namely, that the church of God, under all preceding changes, should have this consideration to encourage her, and maintain her hope, and animate her faith and prayers, from generation to generation, that God has promised, her cause should finally be maintained and prevail in the world.

STUDY QUESTIONS

1. We need to analyze Edwards's view before we judge it one way or another. First, it might appear that Edwards is claiming that all people will ultimately be saved. Thus, we might consider Edwards to be a universalist with respect to the extent of God's redemption. Read his argument again carefully. What can you find in his argument to rebut this accusation?

2. It is clear that Edwards believed that the greatest expansion of Christianity was yet to be. Summarize what Edwards believed about the extent of the gospel's reach and the duration of the rule of Christ's peace on earth.

3. Edwards was a postmillennialist. That is, he believed that the so-called millennium ("by which we must understand a very long time") would come after the kingdom of Christ had overcome all his enemies and subdued all the nations, and the knowledge of the glory of God covered the earth as the waters cover the sea. How would you argue with Edwards against this view? How would you argue in support of it?

4. All Christians believe that one day, whether before Christ returns or after, the whole earth will be subject to him in

perfect peace, bliss, and joy. For Edwards, this was great incentive to pray that God would begin to do it soon. How much a part of your own prayers is this blessed hope? Of the prayers you hear during the service of worship in your church? What might you do to help increase such prayers?

5. Edwards made much use of Psalm 67 in expressing his view. This psalm is a prayer to God for the expansion of the gospel. Take some time to pray through this psalm right now, using the words of the psalm to guide you as you pray God's words back to him. Begin to use this psalm in your daily prayers that God would revive his church and bring awakening to the world.

❊ Chapter 3 ❊

THE COMING GLORY

Edwards continues to paint the scenario of the coming day of glory, in which the blessings of God, embodied chiefly in the Holy Spirit, begin to be more and more in evidence on the earth. He calls his readers to pray that this great day of blessing might come soon.

❊

The future promised advancement of the kingdom of Christ is an event unspeakably happy and glorious. The Scriptures speak of it as a time wherein God and his Son Jesus Christ will be most eminently glorified on earth; a time, wherein God, who till then had *dwelt between the cherubims*—and concealed himself in the holy of holies, in the secret of his tabernacle, behind the *veil*, in the thick darkness—should openly *shine forth, and all flesh should see his glory,* and God's people in *general* have as great a privilege as the *High Priest* alone had once a year, or as Moses had in the mount. A time this, wherein the "temple of God in heaven should be opened, and there should be seen the ark of his testament" (Rev. 11:19); a time, wherein both God will be greatly glorified, and his saints made unspeakably happy in the view of his glory, a time, wherein God's people should not only *once* see the light of God's glory, as Moses, or see it *once a year* with the high priest, but should *dwell and walk continually* in it, and it should be their constant daily light, instead of the light of the sun (Isa. 2:5; Ps. 84:11; Isa. 60:19), which light should be so much more glorious than the light of the sun or moon that "the moon shall be confounded, and the sun ashamed, when the Lord of hosts should reign in mount Zion, and in Jerusalem, before his ancients gloriously" (Isa. 24:23).

THE GLORY OF THAT COMING DAY

A day of increase in knowledge and understanding

It is represented as a time of vast increase of *knowledge* and *understanding,* especially in divine things; a time wherein God would "destroy the face of the covering cast over all people, and the veil spread over all nations" (Isa. 25:7), wherein "the light of the moon shall be as the light of the sun, and the light of the sun seven-fold" (Isa. 25:7). "And the eyes of them that see shall not be dim, and the heart of the rash shall understand knowledge" (Isa. 32:3–4). And they shall no more teach every man his neighbor, and every man his brother, saying, Know the Lord, because they shall all know him from the least to the greatest (Jer. 31:34).

A time of general holiness

It is declared to be a time of general *holiness:* "Thy people shall be all righteous" (Isa. 60:21). A time of prevail-

ing *eminent* holiness, when little *children* shall, in spiritual at-
tainments, be as though they were *a hundred years old* (Isa.
65:20); wherein "he that is feeble among God's people
shall be as David" (Zech. 12:8). A time wherein holiness
should be as it were *inscribed on everything*, on all men's common business and employments, and the common utensils
of life, all shall be dedicated to God, and improved to holy
purposes: "Her merchandise and hire shall be holiness to
the Lord" (Isa. 23:18). "In that day there shall be upon the
bells of the horses, *holiness unto the Lord*; and the pots in the
Lord's house shall be like the bowls before the altar; yea,
every pot in Jerusalem and in Judah shall be holiness unto
the Lord of hosts" (Zech. 14:20–21).

A *time of true Christianity above all*

A time shall come wherein religion and true Christianity shall in every respect be *uppermost* in the world; wherein
God will cause his church to "arise and shake herself from
the dust, and put on her beautiful garments, and sit down
on a throne; and the poor shall be raised from the dust, and
the beggar from the dunghill, and shall be set among
princes, and made to inherit the throne of God's glory"—
a time wherein vital piety shall take possession of thrones
and palaces, and those that are in most exalted stations
shall be eminent in holiness (Isa. 49:23). "And kings shall
be thy nursing fathers, and their queens thy nursing moth-
ers" (Isa. 60:16). "Thou shalt suck the breasts of kings"
(Isa. 60:16). "The daughter of Tyre shall be there with a
gift, the rich among the people shall entreat thy favor." A

time of wonderful *union,* and the most universal peace, love, and sweet harmony; wherein the nations "shall beat their swords into plow-shares," etc., and God will "cause wars to cease to the ends of the earth, and break the bow, and cut the spear in sunder, and burn the chariot in fire; and the mountains shall bring forth peace to God's people, and the little hills by righteousness; wherein the wolf shall dwell with the lamb, etc., and wherein God's people shall dwell in a peaceable habitation, and in sure dwellings, and quiet resting places" (Isa. 32:17–18; 33:20–21).

A *time of unity, beauty, and joy*

A time shall come wherein all *heresies* and false doctrines shall be exploded, and the church of God shall not be rent with a variety of jarring opinions: "The Lord shall be king over all the earth: in that day there shall be one Lord, and his name one" (Zech. 14:9). All superstitious ways of worship shall be abolished, and all agree in worshiping God in his own appointed way, and agreeably to the purity of his institutions: "I will give them one heart and one way, that they may fear me for ever, for the good of them and their children after them" (Jer. 32:39). A time wherein the whole earth shall be united as one holy city, one heavenly family, men of all nations shall as it were dwell together, and sweetly correspond one with another, as brethren and children of the same father; as the prophecies often speak of God's people at that time as the children of God, and brethren one to another, all "appointing over them one head," gathered to one "house of God, to worship the King, the Lord of hosts."

A time approaches wherein this whole great society shall appear in glorious beauty, in genuine amiable Christianity and excellent order, as "a city compact together, the perfection of beauty, and eternal excellency," shining with a reflection of the glory of Jehovah risen upon it, which shall be attractive and ravishing to all kings and nations, and it shall appear "as a bride adorned for her husband." A time of great temporal prosperity; of great health: "The inhabitant shall not say, I am sick" (Isa. 33:24); of long life: "As the days of a tree, are the days of my people" (Isa. 65:22). A time wherein the earth shall be abundantly fruitful (Ps. 67; Isa. 6:23–24; Amos 9:15; and many other places). A time wherein the world shall be delivered from that multitude of sore calamities which before had prevailed (Ezek. 47:20), and there shall be an universal blessing of God upon mankind, in soul and body, and in all their concerns, and all manner of tokens of God's presence and favor, and "God shall rejoice over them, as the bridegroom rejoiceth over his bride, and the mountains shall as it were drop down new wine, and the hills shall flow with milk" (Joel 3:18).

A time of great and universal joy, we are taught to expect, will take place through all the earth, when "from the utmost ends of the earth shall be heard songs, even glory to the righteous," and God's people "shall with joy draw water out of the wells of salvation." God shall "prepare in his holy mountain a feast of fat things, a feast of wines on the lees, of fat things full of marrow, of wines on the lees well refined," which feast is represented as *the marriage supper of the Lamb* (Rev. 19). Yea, the Scriptures represent it not only as a time of universal joy on earth, but extraordinary joy in heaven, among the angels and saints, and the holy apostles and prophets there (Rev. 18:20 and 19:1–9). Yea, the Scriptures represent it as a time of extraordinary rejoicing with Christ himself, the glorious head, in whom all things in heaven and earth shall then be gathered together in one: "The Lord thy God in the midst of thee is mighty; he will save; he will rejoice over thee with joy; he will rest in his love; he will joy over thee with singing" (Zeph. 3:17). And the very fields, trees, and mountains shall then as it were rejoice, and break forth into singing: "Ye shall go out with joy, and be led forth with peace; the mountains and the hills shall break forth before you into singing, and all the trees of the field shall clap their hands" (Isa. 55:12). "Sing, O heavens, for the Lord hath done it; shout ye lower parts of the earth; break forth into singing, ye mountains; O forest, and every tree therein: for the Lord hath redeemed Jacob, and glorified himself in Israel" (Isa. 44:23).

A Time Worth Praying For!

Such being the state of things in this future promised glorious day of the church's prosperity, surely it is worth *praying* for. Nor is there anything whatsoever, if we viewed things aright, for which a regard to the glory of God, a concern for the kingdom and honor of our Redeemer, a love to his people, pity to perishing sinners—love to our fellow-creatures in general, compassion to mankind under their various and sore calamities, a desire of their temporal and spiritual prosperity, love to our country, our neighbors, and friends, yea, and to our own souls—would dispose us to be so much in prayer, as for the dawning of this happy day, and the accomplishment of this glorious event.

The Sum of All Grace and Glory

The sum of the blessings Christ sought, by what he did and suffered in the work of redemption, was the *Holy Spirit*. Thus is the affair of our redemption constituted; *the Father* provides and gives the Redeemer, and the price of redemption is offered to him, and he grants the benefit purchased; *the Son* is the Redeemer who gives the price, and also is the price offered; and the *Holy Spirit* is the grand blessing obtained by the price offered, and bestowed on the redeemed.

The Holy Spirit the sum of all blessings

The Holy Spirit, in his indwelling presence, his influences and fruits, is the sum of all grace, holiness, comfort, and joy; or, in one word, of all the spiritual good Christ *purchased* for men in this world: and is also the sum of all perfection, glory, and eternal joy, that he purchased for them in another world. The Holy Spirit is the subject matter of the promises, both of the eternal covenant of redemption, and also of the covenant of grace. This is the grand subject of the *promises* of the Old Testament, so often recorded in the *prophecies* of Messiah's kingdom; and the chief subject of the promises of the New Testament; and particularly of the covenant of grace delivered by Jesus Christ to his disciples, as his last will and testament, in the fourteenth, fifteenth, and sixteenth chapters of John; the grand legacy that he bequeathed to them, in his last and dying discourse with them. Therefore the Holy Spirit is so often called the *Spirit of promise,* and emphatically, *the promise, the promise of the Father,* and so forth.

The Holy Spirit what Christ received from the Father

This being the great blessing Christ purchased by his labors and sufferings on earth, it was that which he *received of the Father* when he ascended into heaven, and entered into the holy of holies with his own blood, that he might communicate it to those whom he had redeemed: "It is expedient for you, that I go away; but if I depart, I will send him unto you" (John 16:7). "Being by the right hand of God exalted, and having received of the Father the promise of the Holy Ghost, he hath shed forth this which ye now see and hear" (Acts 2:33). This is the sum of those *gifts,* which Christ *received for men, even for the rebellious,* at his ascension; and of the *benefits* Christ obtains for men by his *intercession:* "I will pray the Father, and he shall give you another Comforter, that he may abide with you for ever; even the Spirit of truth" (John 14:16–17). Herein consists Christ's communicative *fullness,* even in his being full of the Spirit; and so full of grace and truth, that we might of *this fullness re-*

ceive, and grace for grace. He is *anointed with the Holy Ghost,* and is *the ointment that goes down from the head* to the members. "God gives the Spirit not by measure unto him, that every member might receive according to the measure of the gift of Christ." This therefore was the great blessing he prayed for in that wonderful *prayer* which he uttered for his disciples and all his future church, the evening before he died (John 17). The blessing he prayed for to the Father, in behalf of his disciples, was the same he had insisted on in his preceding discourse with them; and this, doubtless, was the blessing he prayed for, when, as our High Priest, he *offered up strong crying and tears,* with his blood (Heb. 5:6–7). As for this he shed his blood, for this he also shed tears, and poured out prayers.

The Holy Spirit and the appointed time of salvation

But of all the time we have been speaking of, this is the *chief season* for the bestowment of this blessing; the *main season* of success to all that Christ did and suffered in the work of our redemption. Before this the Spirit of God is given but very sparingly, and but few are saved; but *then* it will be far otherwise; wickedness shall be rare then, as virtue and piety had been before: and undoubtedly, by far the greatest number of them that ever receive the benefits of Christ's redemption, from the beginning of the world to the end of it, will receive it in that time.

This time is represented in Scripture, as the *proper appointed* season of Christ's *salvation;* eminently the elect season, *the accepted time,* and *day of salvation.* "The year of Christ's redeemed" (Isa. 63:4). This period is spoken of as the proper time of the Redeemer's *dominion,* and the reign of his redeeming love, in the second and seventh chapters of *Daniel,* and many other places; the proper time of his *harvest,* or ingathering of his fruits from this fallen world; the appointed day of his triumph over *Satan,* the great destroyer; and the appointed day of his *marriage* with his elect spouse (Rev. 19:7). The time given to the *Sun of righteousness* to rule, as the day is the time God has appointed for the natural sun to bear rule. There the bringing on of this time is called "Christ's coming in his kingdom"; wherein "he will rend the heavens and come down, and the Sun of righteousness shall arise" (Mal. 4:2; Isa. 60:1).

The present a time of anticipation

The comparatively *little* saving good there is in the world, as the fruit of Christ's redemption, before that time, is as it were granted by way of *anticipation;* as we anticipate something of the sun's light by reflection before the proper time of the sun's rule; and as the first-fruits are gathered before the *harvest. Then* more especially will be the fulfillment of those great promises, made by God the Father to the Son, for his pouring out his soul unto death (Isa. 53:10–12): Then "shall he see his seed, and the pleasure of the Lord shall prosper in his hand"; then "shall he see the travail of his soul, and be satisfied, and shall justify many by his knowledge"; then "will God divide him a portion with the great, and he shall divide the spoil with the strong"; then shall Christ in an eminent manner obtain his chosen spouse, that "he loved and died for, that he might sanctify and cleanse her, with the washing of water, by the word, and present her to himself, a glorious church." He will obtain "the joy that was set before him, for which he endured the cross, and despised the shame," chiefly in the events and consequences of that day: that day, as was observed before, which is often represented as eminently the time of the "rejoicing of the bridegroom." The foreknowledge and consideration of it was what supported him, and that in which his soul exulted, at a time when it had been troubled at the view of his approaching sufferings, as may be seen in John 12:23–24, 27, 31–32.

CALL TO PRAYER

Now therefore, if this is what *Jesus Christ*, our great Redeemer and the head of the church, did so much desire, and set his heart upon, from all eternity, and for which he did and suffered so much, offering up *strong crying and tears*, and *his precious blood*, to obtain it; surely his disciples and members should also earnestly seek it, and be much in prayer for it.

STUDY QUESTIONS

1. Let's look at Edwards's argument in this chapter from two points of view: first, Edwards's own. For the sake of argument, let's accept Edwards's postmillennial view of things, his understanding of how the course of history will be unfolding in that great coming day. Summarize the situation

as Edwards saw it and for which he was calling people to unite in prayer.

2. Whether we accept Edwards's postmillennialism or not, every Christian will agree that the blessings he describes are worth striving for. Whatever one's eschatology—postmillennial, premillennial, amillennial, or something else—we all want to see the world know more of the blessings of the gospel. This is why we preach the gospel, send out missionaries, start new churches, take up social and moral causes, and invest in redeeming culture for the glory of God and the good of people. Imagine that through a united, extraordinary effort at prayer, involving your church and other churches, the blessings Edwards envisioned in this section could be more completely realized in your community. What would be different? What would your community look like if more of these blessings could begin to be attained? Is this a vision worth praying for?

3. Now let's spiritualize Edwards's postmillennialism a bit. Read again the paragraph under the heading *The Holy Spirit the sum of all blessings.* Let's assume that all the images Edwards envisioned, and that we summarized under question I above, were just symbolic ways of speaking about the experience of receiving and living in the Holy Spirit. Think of all the Scriptures teach about living in the Spirit. In such a situation, what would a person look like, and what would his or her church be like, where the Spirit of God was present in greater fullness and power? Imagine many

churches in your community so blessed: How might that affect your community? Is *this* a vision worth praying for?

4. Suppose your answers to the last question in number 3 and number 2 above were yes. What might you do to start getting people together to pray for the kind of revival that would issue in such benefits as summarized above? Whom would you invite to join you? Are there any other churches in your community that might be interested in participating? What is keeping you from organizing such an effort?

5. Pray through Psalm 67 again, right now. As you pray, think over the images Edwards presented in this chapter and that you summarized above. Begin to put your heart into this prayer, calling upon God to be faithful *to his own words* and to make his salvation more powerfully known in you, in your church, and in your community. Over the next several days, find one other person who you think might be interested in beginning to meet with you to pray for revival; share your experience of beginning to pray this psalm and what you hope might come out of uniting to pray for revival.

❧ *Chapter 4* ❧

GROANING AND WAITING
IN PRAYER

*In this, the largest section of Edwards's book, he argues for the neces-
sity of earnestly waiting on God in united, extraordinary prayer,
groaning and travailing with all the rest of creation for the glorious
day of revival and renewal which is sure to come.*

❧

The *whole creation* is, as it were, *earnestly waiting* for that
day, and constantly *groaning and travailing in pain* to bring
forth the felicity and glory of it. For that day is above all
other times, excepting the day of judgment, the day of *the
manifestation of the sons of God,* and of their *glorious liberty*: and
therefore that elegant representation the apostle makes of
the earnest expectation and travail of the creation in Romans 8:19–22 is applicable to the glorious event of this
day; "the earnest expectation of the creature waiteth for the
manifestation of the sons of God. For the creature was
made subject to vanity, not willingly, but by reason of him
who hath subjected the same in hope. Because the creature
itself also shall be delivered from the bondage of corrup-

tion into the glorious liberty of the children of God. For we know that the whole creation groaneth and travaileth in pain together until now."

The Effects of Sin

The visible world has now for many ages been subject to *sin,* and made, as it were, a servant to it, through the abuse that man, who has the dominion over the creatures, puts the creatures to. Thus the sun is a sort of servant to all manner of wickedness, as its light, and other beneficial influences, are abused by men, and made subservient to their lusts and sinful purposes. So of the rain, the fruits of the earth, the brute animals, and all other parts of the visible creation; they all serve men's corruption, and obey their sinful will. And God doth, in a sort, subject them to it; for he continues his influence and power to make them obedient, according to the same law of nature, whereby they yield to men's command when used to good purposes.

God's sovereignty over created things

It is by the immediate influence of God upon things according to those constant methods which we call the laws of nature that they are obedient to man's will, or that we can use them at all. This influence God continues in order to make them obedient to man's will, though wicked. This is a sure sign that the present state of things is not lasting: it is confusion; and God would not suffer it to be, but that he designs in a little time to put an end to it. Seeing it is to be but a little while, God chooses rather to subject the creature to man's wickedness than to disturb and interrupt the course of nature according to its stated laws: but it is, as it were, a force upon the creature; for the creature is abused in it, perverted to far meaner purposes, than those for which the author of its nature made and adapted it.

The creature therefore is unwillingly subject; and but for a short time; and, as it were, hopes for an alteration. It is a bondage which the creature is subject to, from which it was partly delivered when Christ came, and when the gospel was promulgated in the world; and will be more fully delivered at the commencement of the glorious day we are speaking of, and perfectly at the day of judgment. This agrees with the context; for the apostle was speaking of the present suffering state of the church. The reason why the church in this world is in a suffering state is that the world is subject to the sin and corruption of mankind. By *vanity and corruption* in Scripture, is very commonly meant sin, or wickedness; as might be shown in very many places, would my intended brevity allow.

The earnest expectation of the creation

Though the creature is thus subject to vanity, yet does not it rest in this subjection, but is constantly acting and exerting itself, in order to that glorious liberty that God has appointed at the time we are speaking of, and, as it were, reaching forth toward it. All the changes brought to pass in the world, from age to age, are ordered by infinite wisdom, in one respect or other to prepare the way for that glorious issue of things, when truth and righteousness shall finally prevail, and he, whose right it is, shall take the kingdom. All the creatures, in all their operations and motions, continually tend to this. As in a clock, all the motions of the whole system of wheels and movements, tend to the striking of the hammer at the appointed time. All the revolutions and restless motions of the sun and other heavenly bodies, from day to day, from year to year, and from age to age, are continually tending thither; as all the many turnings of the wheels of a chariot, in a journey, tend to the appointed journey's end. The mighty struggles and conflicts of nations, those vast successive changes which are brought to pass in the kingdoms and empires of the world, from one age to another, are, as it were, travail-pangs of the creation, in order to bring forth this glorious event. And the Scriptures represent the last struggles and changes that shall immediately precede this event, as being the greatest of all; as the last pangs of a woman in travail are the most violent.

The creature thus earnestly expecting this glorious manifestation and liberty of the children of God, and travailing in pain in order to it, the Scriptures, by a like figure, very often show that when this shall be accomplished, the whole inanimate creation shall greatly rejoice: "That the heavens shall sing, the earth be glad, the mountains break forth into singing, the hills be joyful together, the trees clap their hands, the lower parts of the earth shout, the sea roar and the fullness thereof, and the floods clap their hands."

The saints called to wait and long for this day

All the intelligent elect creation, all God's holy creatures in heaven and earth, are truly and properly waiting
for, and earnestly expecting this event. It is abundantly represented in Scripture as the spirit and character of all true
saints that they set their hearts upon, love, long, wait, and
pray for the promised glory of that day; they are spoken of
as those that "prefer Jerusalem to their chief joy" (Ps.
137:6); "that take pleasure in the stones of Zion, and favor the dust thereof" (Ps. 102:13–14); "that wait for the
consolation of Israel" (Luke 2:25, 38). It is the language
of the church of God, and the breathing of every true saint:
"O that the salvation of Israel were come out of Zion!
When the Lord bringeth back the captivity of the people,
Jacob shall rejoice, and Israel shall be glad" (Ps. 14:7).
And: "Until the day break, and the shadows flee away, turn,
my beloved, and be thou like a roe, or a young hart upon
the mountains of Bether" (Song 2:17). And: "Make haste,
my beloved, and be thou like to a roe, or to a young hart
upon the mountains of spices" (Song 8:14). Agreeable to
this was the spirit of old Jacob, which he expressed when
he was dying, exercising faith in the great promise made to
him, and Isaac, and Abraham, that "in their seed all the
families of the earth should be blessed"; "I have waited for
thy salvation, O Lord" (Gen. 49:18). The same is represented as the spirit of his true children, or the family of Jacob: "I will wait upon the Lord, that hideth himself from
the house of Jacob, and I will look for him" (Isa. 8:17).

"They that love Christ's appearing" is a name that the apostle gives to true Christians (2 Tim. 4:8).

The glorious inhabitants of the heavenly world—the saints and angels there, who rejoice when one sinner repents—are earnestly waiting, in an assured and joyful dependence on God's promises of that conversion of the world and marriage of the Lamb, which shall take place when that glorious day comes: and therefore they are represented as all with one accord rejoicing, and praising God with such mighty exultation and triumph, when it is accomplished (Rev. 19).

INDUCEMENTS TO PRAY

The word of God is full of *precepts, encouragements,* and *examples,* tending to excite and induce the people of God to be much in *prayer* for this mercy.

Seek the Spirit in prayer

The Spirit of God is the *chief* of blessings, for it is the *sum* of all spiritual blessings; which we need infinitely more than others, and wherein our true and eternal happiness consists. That which is the sum of the blessings Christ purchased, is the sum of the blessings Christians have to pray for; but that, as was observed before, is the Holy Spirit. Therefore, when the disciples came to Christ, desiring him to teach them to pray (Luke 11), and he accordingly gave them particular directions for the performance of this duty; he adds, "If ye then, being evil, know how to give good gifts unto your children, how much more shall your heavenly Father give the Holy Spirit to them that ask him?" (Luke 11:13).

From which words of Christ, we may also observe that there is no blessing we have so great encouragement to pray for, as the Spirit of God. The words imply that our heavenly Father is especially ready to bestow his Holy Spirit on them that ask him. The more excellent the nature of any benefit is, which we stand in need of, the more ready God is to bestow it, in answer to prayer. The infinite goodness of God's nature is the more gratified, the grand design of our redemption is the better answered, Jesus Christ, the Redeemer, has the greater success in his undertaking and labors; and those desires which are expressed in prayer for the most excellent blessings, are the most excellent desires, and consequently such as God most approves of, and is most ready to gratify.

The necessity of frequent and importunate prayers

The Scriptures do not only direct and encourage us, in general, to pray for the Holy Spirit above all things else; but it is the expressly revealed will of God that his church should be *very much* in prayer for that glorious outpouring of the Spirit, which is to be in the latter days, and for what shall be accomplished by it. God, speaking of that blessed event (Ezek. 36), under the figure of "cleansing the house of Israel from all their iniquities, planting and building their waste and ruined places, and making them to become like the garden of Eden, and filling them with men like a flock, like the holy flock, the flock of Jerusalem in their solemn feasts," he says. "Thus saith the Lord, I will yet for this be inquired of by the house of Israel, to do it for them" (Ezek. 36:37). Which doubtless implies it is the will of God that extraordinary prayerfulness in his people for this mercy should precede the bestowment of it.

I know of no place in the Bible, where so strange an expression is made of to signify *importunity* in prayer, as is used in Isaiah 57:6–7, where the people of God are called upon to be importunate for this mercy: "Ye that make mention of the Lord, keep not silence, and give him no rest, till he establish and till he make Jerusalem a praise in the earth." How strong is the phrase! And how loud is this call to the church of God, to be fervent and incessant in their cries to him for this great mercy! How wonderful the words used, concerning the manner in which such worms of the dust should address the high and lofty One that inhabits eternity! And what encouragement is here, to approach the mercy-seat with greatest freedom, humble boldness, earnestness, constancy, and full assurance of faith, to seek of God this greatest favor that can be sought in Christian prayer!

The example of the Lord's Prayer

It is a just observation of a certain eminent minister of the church of Scotland, in a discourse lately published on *social prayer,* in which, speaking of pleading for the success of the gospel, as required by the *Lord's Prayer,* he says, "That notwithstanding of its being so compendious, yet the one half of it, that is, three petitions in six, and these the first prescribed, do all relate to this great case: so that to put any one of these petitions apart, or all of them together, is upon the matter, to pray that the dispensation of the gospel may be blessed with divine power."

That glorious day is the proper and appointed time, above all others, for bringing to pass the things requested in each of these petitions. The prophecies everywhere represent *that* as the time, which God has especially appointed for glorifying his own great name in this world, causing "his glory to be revealed, that all flesh may see it together," causing it "openly to be manifested in the sight of the heathen," filling the whole world with the light of his glory to such a degree that "the moon shall be confounded and the sun ashamed" before that brighter glory; the appointed time for glorifying and magnifying the name of Jesus Christ, causing "every knee to bow and every tongue to confess him." This is the proper time *of God's kingdom coming,* or of *Christ's coming in his kingdom:* that is, the very time foretold in the second chapter of Daniel, when the *Lord God of heaven shall set up a kingdom,* in the latter times of the last monarchy, when it is divided into ten kingdoms.

And that is the very time foretold in the seventh chapter of Daniel, when there should be "given to one like the Son of man, dominion, glory, and a kingdom, that all people, nations and languages should serve them; and the kingdom and dominion, and the greatness of the kingdom, under the whole of heaven, shall be given to the people of the saints of the most high God," after the destruction of

the *little horn,* that should come *for a time, times, and the divid-
ing of* time. And that is the time wherein "God's will shall
be done on earth, as it is done in heaven"; when *heaven* shall,
as it were, be *bowed,* and *come down* to the earth, as "God's
people shall be all righteous, *and* holiness to the Lord shall
be written on the bells of horses," and so forth. So that the
three first petitions of the Lord's Prayer are, in effect, no
other than requests for bringing on this glorious day. And
as the Lord's Prayer begins with asking for this, in the first
three petitions, so it concludes with it in these words, "For
thine is the kingdom, and the power, and the glory, for ever.
Amen." Which words imply a request that God would take
to himself his great power, and reign, and manifest his
power and glory in the world.

Thus Christ teaches us that it becomes his disciples to
seek this above all other things, and make it the first and
last in their prayers, and that every petition should be put
up in subordination to the advancement of God's kingdom
and glory in the world.

Prayers for the revival of the church of preeminence in Scripture

Besides what has been observed of the Lord's Prayer, if
we look through the whole Bible, and observe all the *examples* of prayer that we find there recorded, we shall not find
so many prayers for any other mercy, as for the deliverance,
restoration, and prosperity of the *church,* and the advancement of *God's glory* and *kingdom of grace* in the world. If we
well consider the prayers recorded in the book of *Psalms,* I
believe we shall see reason to think that a very great, if not

the greater, part of them, are prayers uttered, either in the name of *Christ,* or in the name of the *church,* for such a mercy: and undoubtedly, the greatest part of the book of *Psalms* is made up of prayers for this mercy, prophecies of it, and prophetical praises for it.

In order to Christ being mystically born, in the advancement of true religion, and the great increase of true converts, who are spoken of as having *Christ formed in them,* the Scriptures represent it as requisite that the *church* should first be "in travail, crying in pain to be delivered" (Rev. 12:1–2, 5). And we have good reason to understand by it here exercising strong desires, wrestling and agonizing with God in *prayer,* for this event; because we find such figures of speech used in this sense elsewhere: "My little children, of whom I travail in birth again, until Christ be formed in you" (Gal. 4:19). "Lord, in trouble have they visited thee; they poured out a prayer when thy chastening was upon them. Like a woman with child, that draweth near the time of her delivery, is in pain, and crieth out in her pangs, so have we been in thy sight, O Lord" (Isa. 26:16–17). And certainly it is fit, that the *church* of God should be in travail for that for which the whole *creation* travails in pain.

The prospects of success

The Scripture does not only abundantly manifest it to be the duty of God's people to be much in prayer for this great mercy, but it also abounds with manifold considerations to *encourage* them in it, and animate them with hopes of *success*. There is perhaps no one thing that the Bible so promises, in order to encourage faith, hope, and prayers of the saints, as this; which affords to God's people the clearest evidences that it is their *duty* to be much in prayer for this mercy. For, undoubtedly, that which God abundantly makes the subject of his *promises,* God's people should abundantly make the subject of their *prayers*. It also affords them the strongest assurance that their prayers shall be *successful*. With that confidence may we go before God, and pray for that of which we have so many exceeding precious and glorious promises to plead! The very *first* promise of God to fallen man (Gen. 3:15), *It shall bruise thy head,* is to have its chief fulfillment at *that day*. And the whole Bible *concludes* with a promise of the glory of *that day,* and a prayer for its fulfillment: "He that testifieth these things saith, Surely I come quickly; Amen. Even so, come, Lord Jesus" (Rev. 22:20).

The Scripture gives us great reason to think that once there comes to appear much of a *spirit of prayer* in the church of God for this mercy, then it will soon be accomplished. It is evidently with reference to this mercy that God makes the promise in Isaiah 41:17–19: "When the poor and needy seek water and there is none, and their tongue faileth them for thirst, I, the Lord, will hear them; I, the God of *Israel,* will not forsake them; I will open rivers in high places, and fountains in the midst of the valleys; I will make the wilderness a pool of water, and the dry land springs of water, I will plant in the wilderness the cedar, the shittah-tree, and the myrtle, and the oil-tree; I will set in

the desert the fir-tree, the pine, and the box-tree together."
Spiritual *waters* and *rivers* are explained by the apostle John,
to be the *Holy Spirit* (John 7:37–39). It is now a time of
scarcity of these spiritual waters; there are, as it were, *none*.
If God's people, in this time of great drought, were but
made sensible of this calamity, and their own emptiness
and necessity, and brought earnestly to *thirst* and *cry* for
needed supplies, God would, doubtless, soon fulfill this
blessed promise. We have another promise much like this,
in Psalm 102:16–17: "When the Lord shall build up *Zion,*
he shall appear in his glory; he will regard the prayer of the
destitute, and not despise their prayer." And remarkable are
the words that follow in the next verse: "This shall be written for the generation to come; and the people which shall
be created, shall praise the Lord." Which seems to signify
that this promise shall be left on record to encourage some
future generation of God's people to pray and cry earnestly
for this mercy, to whom he would *fulfill* the promise, and
thereby give them, and great multitudes of others who
should be converted through their prayers, occasion to
praise his name.

Who knows but that the generation here spoken of,
may be this *present* generation? *One* thing mentioned in the
character of that future generation, is certainly true concerning the present, namely, that it is *destitute.* The church
of God is in very low, sorrowful, and needy circumstances;
and if the *next* thing there supposed were also verified in us,
namely, that we were made *sensible* of our great calamity, and
brought to *cry earnestly* to God for help, I am persuaded the

third would also be verified, namely, that our *prayers* would be turned into joyful *praise,* for God's gracious answers of them. It is spoken of as a sign and evidence that *the time to favor* Zion *is come,* when God's *servants* are brought by their prayerfulness for her restoration, in an eminent manner, to show that they *favor her stones and dust:* "Thou shalt arise, and have mercy upon *Zion;* for the time to favor her, yea, the set time, is come; for thy servants take pleasure in her stones, and favor the dust thereof" (Ps. 102:13–14).

Prayer and God's government of the world

God has *respect* to the *prayers* of his saints in all his *government* of the *world;* as we may observe by the representation made [in] Revelation 8, at the beginning. There we read of *seven angels* standing before the throne of God, and receiving of him *seven trumpets,* at the sounding of which, great and mighty changes were to be brought to pass in the world, through many successive ages. But when these angels had received their trumpets, they must stand still, and all must be in silence, not one of them must be allowed to *sound,* till the *prayers of the saints* are attended to. The angel of the covenant, as a glorious high priest, comes and stands at the altar, with much incense, to offer with the *prayers of all saints* upon the golden altar, before the throne; and the smoke of the incense, with the *prayers of the saints,* ascends up with acceptance before God, out of the angel's hand: and *then* the angels prepare themselves to sound. And God, in the events of every trumpet, remembers those *prayers:* as appears at last, by the great and glorious things he accomplishes for his church, in the issue of all, in *answer* to these prayers, in the event of the *last trumpet,* which brings the glory of the *latter days,* when these prayers shall be turned into *joyful praises.* "And the seventh angel sounded; and there were great voices in heaven, saying, The kingdoms of this world are become the kingdoms of our Lord and of his Christ and he shall reign for ever and ever. And the four-and-twenty elders, which sat before God on their seats, fell upon their faces, and worshiped God, saying, We give thee thanks, O Lord God Almighty, which art and wast and art to come because thou has taken to thee thy great power, and hast reigned" (Rev. 11:15–17).

Since it is the pleasure of God so to honor his people, as to carry on all the designs of his kingdom in this way, namely, by the prayers of the saints, this gives us great reason to think that whenever the time comes that God gives an extraordinary spirit of prayer for the promised advancement of his kingdom on earth—which is God's great aim in all preceding providences, and the main thing that the spirit of prayer in the saints aims at—then the fulfillment of this event is nigh.

God stands ready to answer us when we pray

God, in wonderful grace, is pleased to represent himself, as it were, *at the command* of his people with regard to mercies of this nature, so as to be ready to bestow them whenever they earnestly pray for them: "Thus saith the Lord, the Holy One of Israel, and his Maker, Ask me of things to come concerning my sons, and concerning the work of my hands, command ye me" (Isa. 45:11). What God is speaking of, in this context, is the restoration of his church; not only a restoration from temporal calamity and an outward captivity, by *Cyrus;* but also a spiritual restoration and advancement, by God's commanding the heavens to "drop down from above, and the skies to pour down righteousness, and causing the earth to open and bring forth salvation, and righteousness to spring up together" (Isa. 45:8). God would have his people ask of him, or inquire of him by earnest prayer, to do this for them; and manifests himself as being at the command of earnest prayers for such a mercy: and a reason why God is so ready to hear such prayer is couched in the words, because it is prayer for his own church, his chosen and beloved people, "his sons and daughters, and the work of his hands"; and he cannot deny anything that is asked for their comfort and prosperity.

God speaks of himself as standing ready to be *gracious* to his church, and to appear for its restoration, and only *waiting* for such an opportunity to bestow this mercy, when he shall hear the cries of his people for it, that he may bestow it in answer to their prayers: "Therefore will the Lord wait, that he may be gracious to thee: and therefore will he be exalted, that he may have mercy upon you; for the Lord is a God of judgment: blessed are all they that wait for him. For the people shall dwell in Zion at Jerusalem. Thou shalt weep no more; he will be very gracious unto thee, at the voice of thy cry; when he shall hear it, he will answer thee" (Isa. 30:18–19). The words imply that when God sees his people much engaged in praying for this mercy, it shall be no longer delayed. Christ desires to "hear the voice of his spouse, who is in the clefts of the rock, in the secret places of the stairs," in a low and obscure state, driven into secret corners; he only waits for this, in order to put an end to her state of affliction, and cause "the day to break, and the shadows to flee away." If he once heard her voice in earnest prayer, he would come swiftly over the *mountains of separation* between him and her, *as a roe, or young hart* (Song 2:14, etc.).

When his church is in a low state, and oppressed by her enemies, and cries to him, he will swiftly fly to her relief, *as birds fly* at the cry of their young (Isa. 31:5). Yea, when that glorious day comes, "before they call, he will answer them, and while they are yet speaking, he will hear," and in answer to their prayers, he will make "the wolf and the lamb feed together," etc. (Isa. 45:24–25). When the spouse prays for the effusion of the Holy Spirit, and the coming of Christ, by granting the tokens of his spiritual presence in the church, "Awake, O north wind, and come, thou south, blow upon my garden, that the spices of it may flow out; let my beloved come into his garden, and eat his pleasant fruits" (Song 4:16), there seems to be an immediate answer to her prayer, in the next words, in abundant communications of the Spirit, and bestowment of spiritual blessings: "I am come into my garden, my sister, my spouse; I have gathered my myrrh with my spice; I have eaten my honey-comb with my honey; I have drunk my wine with my milk. Eat, O friends; drink, yea, drink abundantly, O beloved" (Song 5:1).

Deliverances of the church in Scripture

Scripture instances and examples of *success* in prayer give great encouragement to pray for this mercy. Most of the remarkable deliverances and restorations of the church of God, mentioned in the Scriptures, were in answer to prayer. For instance, the redemption of the church of God from the *Egyptian* bondage. It was in answer to prayer that the sun stood still over *Gibeon,* and the moon in the valley of *Aijalon,* and God's people obtained that great victory over their enemies; in which wonderful miracle, God seemed to have some respect of a future more glorious event to be accomplished for the Christian church, in the day of her victory over her enemies, in the latter days; even that event foretold: "Thy sun shall no more go down, neither shall thy moon withdraw itself" (Isa. 60:20).

It was in answer to prayer that God delivered his church from the mighty hosts of the *Assyrians,* in Hezekiah's time; which dispensation is a type of the great things God will do for the Christian church in the latter days. The restoration of the church of God from the *Babylonish* captivity, as abundantly appears both by Scripture prophecies, and histories, was in answer to extraordinary prayer. This restoration of the Jewish church, after the destruction of Babylon, is evidently a type of the glorious restoration of the Christian church, after the destruction of the kingdom of *antichrist;* which is abundantly spoken of in the revelation of St. John, as the antitype[1] of *Babylon*. Samson out of weakness received strength to pull down Dagon's temple, through prayer. So the people of God, in the latter days, will out of weakness be made strong, and will become the instruments of pulling down the kingdom of Satan by prayer.

The Spirit of God was poured out upon Christ himself, in answer to prayer: "Now when all the people were baptized, it came to pass, that Jesus also being baptized, and *praying*, the heaven was opened, and the Holy Ghost descended in a bodily shape, like a dove, upon him; and a voice came from heaven, which said, Thou art my beloved Son, in thee I am well pleased" (Luke 3:21–22). The Spirit descends on the church of Christ, the same way, in this respect, that it descended on the head of the church. The greatest effusion of the Spirit that ever yet has been, even that which was in the primitive times of the Christian church, which began in Jerusalem, on the day of *Pentecost*, was in answer to extraordinary prayer. When the disciples were gathered together to their Lord, a little before his ascension, "he commanded them that they should not depart from Jerusalem, but wait for the promise of the Father, which, saith he, ye have heard of me," i.e., the promise of the Holy Ghost (Acts 1:4). What they had their hearts upon was the restoration of the kingdom of Israel: "Lord, (say they) wilt thou at this time restore again the kingdom

1. An antitype is that which fulfills what a type symbolizes, as Jesus was the antitype of the Passover lamb.

to Israel?" (Acts 1:6). And according to Christ's direction, after his ascension, they returned to Jerusalem, and continued in *united fervent prayer* and supplication. It seems they spent their time in it from day to day, without ceasing; till the Spirit came down in a wonderful manner upon them, and that work was begun which never ceased, and all the chief nations were converted to Christianity.

And that glorious deliverance and advancement of the Christian church, that was in the days of *Constantine the Great,* followed the extraordinary cries of the church of God, as the matter is represented at the opening of the fifth seal (Rev. 6). The church in her suffering state, is represented crying with a loud voice, "How long, Lord, holy and true, dost thou not judge, and avenge our blood on them that dwell on the earth?" And the opening of the next seal brings on that mighty revolution, in the days of *Constantine,* compared to those great changes at the end of the world.

GOD WILL COME TO THOSE WHO SEEK HIM

As there is so great and manifold reason from the word of God, to think that if a spirit of earnest prayer for that great effusion of the Spirit of God which I am speaking of, prevailed in the Christian church, the mercy would be soon granted; so those that are engaged in such prayer might well expect the first benefit. God will come to those that are seeking him and waiting for him (Isa. 25:9; 26:8).

When Christ came in the flesh, he was first revealed to them who were *waiting for the consolation of* Israel, and *looking for redemption in* Jerusalem (Luke 1:25). And in that great outpouring of the Spirit that was in the days of the apostles, which was attended with such glorious effects among the Jews and Gentiles, the Spirit came down first on those that were engaged in united earnest prayer for it. A special blessing is promised to them that love and pray for the prosperity of the church of God. "Pray for the peace of Jerusalem. They shall prosper that love thee" (Ps. 137:6).

STUDY QUESTIONS

1. The emphasis in this chapter is on the necessity of "groaning and travailing" in prayer for God to bring the promised season of renewal and blessing. Besides those two terms, how many other different terms or phrases does Edwards use in this chapter to describe the kind of prayers the church needs to engage in? Review this chapter quickly, and make a list of all those words.

2. Now, take all those words and phrases together and, in one sentence, define the kind of prayer to which the church must give itself if God is to pour out his blessings in revival in our day. On a scale of 1 to 10, 10 being the highest rating, how would you rate your prayers for revival in the light of the sentence you wrote? How about the prayers of your church?

3. Edwards suggests that the Psalms are a good place to look for beginning to pray for revival. We have already seen that in Psalm 67. Now let's look at Psalm 80. Here the repeated refrain is for God to pour out his Spirit ("shine his face," cf. Ezek. 39:29) and restore and save his people. Look that psalm over briefly. What aspects of that psalm seem to describe the state of the church today? Which aspects need to be in place before God will revive her? Add this psalm to Psalm 67 as part of your daily prayer for revival.

4. Edwards insists that our prayers, if God is to hear and revive us, must be united, extraordinary, and specific. You have begun to define what that might look like (questions 1 and 2 above). Are there any groups in your church that you might speak to about the challenge of giving at least part of their time to such prayer? How would you approach them? What would it look like if many or even all such groups in your church began to make such prayer part of their regular time together?

5. Review the goals you set for this study in question 5 after chapter 1. Are you making any progress in realizing these? Do you want to revise any of these goals?

❈ *Chapter 5* ❈

THE WITNESS OF DIVINE PROVIDENCE

Edwards shows, by a survey of contemporary crises and calamities, the depraved moral state of the world, and the desperate condition of the churches, that the need is great for God's people to turn to him in prayer for revival.

❈

We are presented with many motives, in the dispensation of divine *providence,* at this day, to excite us to be much in prayer for this mercy. There is much in providence to show us our *need* for it, and put us on *desiring* it. The great outward calamities, in which the world is involved; and particularly the bloody war[1] that embroils and wastes the nations of Christendom, and in which our nation has so great a share, may well make all that believe God's word, and love

1. At that time, England and its colonies were at war with France, and New England fretted constantly, not without reason, about an invasion from Canada and French-incited attacks by Native Americans.

mankind, earnestly long and pray for that day, when the wolf shall lie down with the lamb, and the nations shall beat their swords into plow-shares.

SPIRITUAL CALAMITIES AND MISERIES

But especially do the spiritual calamities and miseries of the present time, show our need of that blessed effusion of God's Spirit: there having been, for so long a time, a great withholding of the Spirit, from the greater part of the Christian world, and such dismal consequences of it in the great decay of vital piety, and the exceeding prevalence of infidelity, heresy, and all manner of vice and wickedness.

Of luxury and vice

Of this a most affecting account has lately been published in a pamphlet, printed in *London*, and reprinted in *Scotland*, entitled *Britain's Remembrancer*; by which it seems that luxury, and wickedness of almost every kind, is well nigh come to the utmost extremity in the nation; and if vice should continue to prevail and increase for one generation more, as it has the generation past, it looks as though the nation could hardly continue in being, but must sink under the weight of its own corruption and wickedness.

And the state of things in other parts of the *British* dominions, besides *England*, is very deplorable. The church of

Scotland has very much lost her glory, greatly departing from her ancient purity, and excellent order; and has of late been bleeding with great and manifold wounds, occasioned by their divisions and hot contentions. And there are frequent complaints from thence, by those that lament the corruptions of that land, of sin and wickedness of innumerable kinds, abounding and prevailing of late, among all ranks of men.

And how lamentable is the moral and religious state of these *American* colonies! Of *New England* in particular! How much is that kind of religion which was professed, much experience, and practice, in the *first* and apparently *best* times in *New England,* grown and growing out of credit! What fierce and violent contentions have been of late among ministers and people, about things of a religious nature! How much is the gospel-ministry grown into contempt! And the work of the ministry, in many respects, laid under uncommon difficulties, and even in danger of sinking among us! How many of our congregations and churches rending in pieces! Church discipline weakened, and ordinances less and less regarded! What wild and extravagant notions, gross delusions of the devil, and strange practices have prevailed, and do still prevail in many places, under a pretext of extraordinary purity, spirituality, liberty, and zeal against formality, usurpation, and conformity to the world! How strong, deeply rooted, and general, are the prejudices that prevail against vital religion and the power of godliness, and almost everything that appertains to it, or tends to it! How apparently are the hearts of people, everywhere, uncommonly shut up against all means and endeavors to awaken sinners and revive religion! Vice and immorality, of all kinds, withal increasing and unusually prevailing! May not an attentive view and consideration of such a state of things well influence the people that favor the dust of *Zion,* to earnestness in their cries to God for a general outpouring of his Spirit, which alone can be an effectual remedy for these evils?

Fresh efforts by anti-Christian powers

Besides, the fresh attempts made by the anti-Christian powers against the protestant interest, in their late endeavors to restore a popish government in *Great Britain,* the chief bulwark of the protestant cause; as also the persecution lately revived against the protestants in *France;* may well give occasion to the people of God, to renewed and extraordinary earnestness in their prayer to him, for the fulfillment of the promised downfall of antichrist, and that liberty and glory of his church that shall follow.

PROVIDENTIAL ENCOURAGEMENT

As there is much in the present state of things to show us our great need of this mercy, and to cause us to desire it; so there is very much to convince us that *God alone can bestow it;* and show us our entire and absolute dependence on him for it.

Human weakness and inability

The insufficiency of human abilities to bring to pass any such happy change in the world as is foretold, or to afford any remedy to mankind from such miseries as have been mentioned does now remarkably appear. Those observations of the apostle, "The world by wisdom knows not God, and God makes foolish the wisdom of the world" (I Cor. I:18–19), never were verified to such a degree as they are now. Great discoveries have been made in the arts and sciences, and never was human learning carried to such a height, as in the present age; and yet never did the cause of religion and virtue run so low, in nations professing true religion. Never was there an age wherein so many learned and elaborate treatises have been written, in proof of the truth and divinity of the Christian religion; yet never were there so many infidels, among those that were brought up under the light of the gospel.

It is an age, as is supposed, of great light, freedom of thought, discovery of truth in matters of religion, detection of the weakness and bigotry of our ancestors, and of the folly and absurdity of the notions of those who were accounted eminent divines in former generations; which notions, it is imagined, destroyed the very foundations of virtue and religion, and enervated all precepts of morality, and in effect annulled all difference between virtue and vice; and yet vice and wickedness did never so prevail, like an overflowing deluge. It is an age wherein those mean and stingy principles, as they are called, of our forefathers, which are supposed to have deformed religion, and led to unworthy thoughts of God, are very much discarded and grown out of credit, and thoughts of the nature of religion, and of the Christian scheme, supposed to be more free, noble, and generous, are entertained. But yet never was there an age, wherein religion in general was so much despised and trampled on, and Jesus Christ and God Almighty so blasphemed and treated with open, daring contempt.

The exceeding *weakness* of mankind, and their *insufficiency* in themselves for bringing to pass anything great and good in the world, with regard to its moral and spiritual state, remarkably appears in many things that have attended and followed the extraordinary religious commotion, that has lately been in many parts of *Great Britain* and *America*. The infirmity of human nature has been manifested, in a very affecting manner, in the various passions of men, and the innumerable ways in which they have been moved, as a reed shaken with the wind, on occasion of the changes and incidents, both public and private, of such a state of things. How many errors and extremes are we liable to! How quickly blinded, misled, and confounded! And how easily does *Satan* make fools of men, if confident in their own wisdom and strength, and left to themselves! Many, in the late wonderful season,[2] were ready to admire and trust in men, as if all depended on such and such instruments; at least, ascribed too much to their skill and zeal, because

2. He is referring to what we call the Great Awakening of the early 1740s.

God was pleased to employ them a little while to do extraordinary things; but what great things does the skill and zeal of instruments do now, when the Spirit of God is withdrawn?

Darkness before dawn

As the present state of things may well excite earnest desires after the promised general revival and advancement of true religion, and serve to show our dependence on God for it, so there are many things in *providence,* of late, that tend to *encourage* us in prayer for such a mercy. That infidelity, heresy, and vice do so prevail, and that corruption and wickedness are risen to such an extreme height, is exceeding deplorable; but yet, I think, considering God's promises to his church, and the ordinary method of his dispensations, hope may justly be gathered from it, that the present state of things will not last long, but that a happy change is nigh. We know that God never will desert the cause of truth and holiness, nor suffer the gates of hell to prevail against the church; and that usually, from the beginning of the world, the state of the church has appeared most dark, just before some remarkable deliverance and advancement. "Many a time, may Israel say, Had not the Lord been on our side, then our enemies would have swallowed us up quick. The waters had overwhelmed us." The church's extremity has often been God's opportunity for magnifying his power, mercy, and faithfulness toward her. The interest of vital piety has long been in general decaying, and error and wickedness prevailing; it looks as though the disease were now come to a crisis, and that things cannot remain long in such a state, but that a change may be expected in one respect or other.

Present and late providences

And not only God's manner of dealing with his church in former ages, and many things in the promises and prophecies of his word, but also several things appertaining to present and late aspects of divine providence, seem to give reason to hope that the change will be such, as to magnify God's free grace and sovereign mercy, and not his revenging justice and wrath. There are certain times, which are days of vengeance, appointed for the more special displays of God's justice and indignation. God has also his days of mercy, accepted times, chosen seasons, wherein it is his pleasure to show mercy, and nothing shall hinder it; times appointed for the magnifying of the Redeemer and his merits, and for the triumphs of his grace, wherein his grace shall triumph over men's unworthiness in its greatest height. And if we consider God's late dealings with our nation and this land, it appears to me that there is much to make us think that this is such a day.

God's patience was very wonderful of old, toward the ten tribes, and the people of Judah and Jerusalem, and afterwards to the Jews in the times of Christ and the apostles; but it seems to me, all things considered, not equal to his patience and mercy to us. God does not only forbear to destroy us, notwithstanding all our provocations, but he has wrought great things for us, wherein his hand has been most visible, and his arm made bare; especially these two instances in *America,* God succeeding us against *Cape-Breton,* and confounding the Armada from *France* the last year;[3] dispensations of providence, which, if considered in all their circumstances, were so wonderfully and apparently manifesting an extraordinary divine interposition that they come perhaps the nearest to a parallel with God's wonderful works of old, in the times of Moses, Joshua, and Hezekiah, of any that have been in these latter ages of the world. And it is to my present purpose to observe that God was pleased to do great things for us in both these instances, in answer to *extraordinary prayer.* Such remarkable appearances of a spirit of prayer, on any particular public occasion, have not been in the land, at any time within my observation and memory, as on the occasion of the affair of *Cape-Breton.* And it is worthy to be remembered that God sent that great storm on the fleet of our enemies the last year that finally dispersed and utterly confounded them, and caused them wholly to give over their designs against us, the very night after our day of public fasting and prayer, for our protection and their confusion.

Thus, although it be a day of great apostasy and provocation, yet it is apparently a day of the wonderful works of God; wonders of power and mercy; which may well lead us to think on those two places of Scripture: "It is time for thee, Lord, to work, for they have made void thy law" (Ps. 119:126) and "that thy name is near thy wondrous works

3. Two significant victories in England's war with France.

declare" (Ps. 75:1). God appears, as it were, loth to destroy us, or deal with us according to our iniquities, great and aggravated as they are; and shows that mercy pleases him. Though a corrupt time, it is plain, by experience, that it is a time wherein God may be found, and he stands ready to show mercy in answer to prayer. He that has done such great things, and has so wonderfully and speedily answered prayer for temporal mercies, will much more give the Holy Spirit if we ask him. He marvelously preserves us, and waits to be gracious to us, as though he chose to make us monuments of his grace, and not of his vengeance, and waits only to have us open our mouths wide, that he may fill them.

Religious awakenings

The late remarkable *religious awakenings,* in many parts of the Christian world, may justly encourage us in prayer for the promised glorious and universal outpouring of the Spirit of God. "About the year 1732 or 1733, God was pleased to pour out his Spirit on the people of *Saltzburg* in *Germany,* who were living under popish darkness, in a most uncommon manner; so that above twenty thousand of them, merely by reading the Bible, which they made a shift to get in their own language, were determined to throw off popery, and embrace the reformed religion; yea, and to become so very zealous for the truth and gospel of Jesus Christ, as to be willing to suffer the loss of all things in the world, and actually to forsake their houses, lands, goods, and relations that they might enjoy the pure preaching of the gospel: with great earnestness, and tears in their eyes, beseeching protestant ministers to preach to them, in different places where they came, when banished from their own country." In the year 1734 and 1735, there appeared a very great and general awakening, in the county of *Hampshire*, in the province of Massachusetts Bay, in New England, and also in many parts of Connecticut. Since this, there has been a far more extensive awakening of many thousands in England, Wales, and Scotland, and almost all the British provinces in North America. There has also been something remarkable of the same kind, in places in the united Netherlands; and about two years ago, a very great awakening and reformation of many of the Indians, in the Jerseys, and Pennsylvania, even among such as never embraced Christianity before: and within these two years, a great awakening in Virginia and Maryland.

Notwithstanding the great diversity of opinions about the issue of some of these awakenings, yet I know of none, who have denied that there have been great awakenings of late, in these times and places, and that multitudes have been brought to more than common concern for their salvation, and for a time were made more than ordinarily afraid of sin, and brought to reform their former vicious courses, and take much pains for their salvation. If I should be of the opinion of those who think that these awakenings and striving of God's Spirit have been generally not well improved, and so, as to most, have ended in enthusiasm and delusion; yet that the Spirit of God has been of late so wonderfully striving with such multitudes—in so many different parts of the world, and even to this day, in one place or other, continues to awaken men—is what I should take great encouragement from, that God was about to do something more glorious, and would, before he finishes, bring things to a greater ripeness, and not finally suffer this work to be frustrated and rendered abortive by *Satan's* crafty management. And may we not hope, that these unusual commotions are the forerunners of something exceeding glorious approaching; as the wind, earthquake, and fire at mount *Sinai,* were forerunners of the voice wherein God was in a more eminent manner? (1 Kings 19:11–12).

STUDY QUESTIONS

1. Read back through this chapter quickly. In the margin, make a note each time something Edwards notes calls to mind some situation we are experiencing today.

2. Given what you see, would you agree that our nation today and the church in our nation are ripe for a period of God's renewed blessing? Explain.

3. Let's take a look at another psalm. Psalm 44 is another excellent psalm to use in praying for revival. Which verses in Psalm 44 remind you of things you have read in this chapter? Take the time right now to pray through this psalm, as you are doing with Psalm 67 and Psalm 80.

4. Edwards only hints at this, but what is the alternative to God *not* bringing revival to his church at this time? What do you suppose that might look like? In view of that, is it worthwhile to try to organize a united, extraordinary effort to pray for revival?

5. Is your practice of prayer being affected by what you have read thus far? Why or why not? What obstacles are in your life to keep you from becoming more consistent in praying for revival? In joining with others to pray for revival? Are you willing to remove those obstacles?

❊ Chapter 6 ❊
THE BEAUTY OF UNION IN PRAYER

In this brief section Edwards argues that our prayers for revival must be united; that is, we must gather together and be in explicit agreement for the concerns about which we are praying. Such united agreement in prayer is beautiful, profitable, and according to the teaching and example of Scripture.

How *condecent,* how *beautiful,* and of *good tendency* it would be, for multitudes of Christians, in various parts of the world, by *explicit agreement,* to unite in such prayer as is proposed to us. *Union* is one of the most *amiable* things that pertains to human society; yea, it is one of the most beautiful and happy things on earth, which indeed makes earth most like heaven. God has made of one blood all nations of men, to dwell on all the face of the earth; hereby teaching us this moral lesson, that it becomes mankind all to be united as one family. And this is agreeable to the nature God has given men, disposing them to society; and the circumstances in which he has placed them, so many ways obliging and necessitating them to it. A *civil* union, or an harmonious agreement among men in the management of their secular concerns, is amiable; but much more a *pious* union, and sweet agreement in the great business for which man was created, even the business of religion; the life and soul of which is LOVE.

THE PECULIAR BEAUTY OF THE CHURCH

Union is spoken of in Scripture as the peculiar beauty of the church of Christ: "My dove, my undefiled, is but one, she is the only one of her mother, she is the choice one of her that bare her; the daughters saw her and blessed her, yea, the queens and the concubines, and they praised her" (Song 6:9). "Jerusalem is builded as a city that is compact together" (Ps. 122:3). "Endeavoring to keep the unity of the Spirit in the bond of peace. There is one body, and one Spirit, even as ye are called in one hope of your calling; one Lord, one faith, one baptism, one God and Father of all, who is above all, and through all, and in you all" (Eph. 4:3–6). "The whole body fitly framed together and compacted, by that which every joint supplieth, according to the effectual working in the measure of every part, maketh increase of the body, unto the edifying of itself in love" (Eph. 4:16).

To be beautiful unity must be manifest
As it is the glory of the church of Christ that in all her members, however dispersed, she is thus *one,* one holy soci-

ety, one city, one family, one body; so it is very desirable that this union should be *manifested,* and become visible. It is highly desirable that here distant members should act as *one,* in those things that concern the common interest of the whole body, and in those duties and exercises wherein they have to do with their common Lord and Head, as seeking of him the common prosperity. As it becomes all the members of a particular family, who are strictly united, and have in so many respects one common interest, to unite in prayer to God for the things they need; and as it becomes a nation, at certain seasons, visibly to unite in prayer for those public mercies that concern the interest of the whole nation: so it becomes the church of Christ—which is one holy nation, a peculiar people, one heavenly family, more strictly united, in many respects, and having infinitely greater interests that are common to the whole, than any other society—visibly to unite and expressly to agree together, in prayer to God for the *common prosperity;* and above all, that common prosperity and advancement, so unspeakably great and glorious, which God hath so abundantly promised to fulfill in the latter days.

It becomes Christians, with whose character a narrow selfish spirit, above all others, disagrees, to be much in prayer for that public mercy, wherein consists the welfare and happiness of the whole body of Christ, of which they are members, and the greatest good of mankind. And union or agreement in prayer is especially becoming, when Christians pray for that mercy, which above all other things concerns them unitedly, and tends to the relief, prosperity, and glory of the whole body, as well as of each individual member.

Visible union in prayer not only beautiful but profitable

Such a union in prayer for the general outpouring of the Spirit of God, would not only be beautiful, but *profitable* too. It would tend very much to promote union and charity between distant members of the church of Christ, to promote public spirit, love to the church of God, and concern for the interest of *Zion*; as well as be an amiable exercise and manifestation of such a spirit.

Union in religious duties, especially in the duty of prayer, in praying one with and for another, and jointly for their common welfare, above almost all other things, tends to promote mutual affection and endearment. And if ministers and people should, by particular agreement and joint resolution, set themselves, in a solemn and extraordinary manner from time to time, to pray for the revival of religion in the world, it would naturally tend more to awaken in them a concern about things of this nature, and more of a desire after such a mercy. It would engage them to more attention to such an affair, make them more inquisitive about it, more ready to use endeavors to promote what they, with so many others, spend so much time in praying for. It would make them more ready to rejoice, and praise God, when they see or hear of anything of that nature or tendency. And, in a particular manner, it would naturally tend to engage ministers—the business of whose lives it should be, to seek the welfare of the church of Christ, and the advancement of his kingdom—to greater diligence and earnestness in their work; and it would have a tendency to the spiritual profit and advantage of each particular person. For persons to be thus engaged in extraordinary prayer for the revival and flourishing state of religion in the world, will naturally lead each one to reflect on *himself*, and consider how religion flourishes in his own heart, and how far his example contributes to that for which he is praying.

SCRIPTURAL ENCOURAGEMENT TO UNITED PRAYER

On the whole there is great and particular *encouragement* given in the word of God, to express *union* and *agreement* in prayer.

The witness of the Old Testament

Daniel, when he had a great thing to request of God, namely, that he by his Holy Spirit would miraculously reveal to him a great secret, which none of the wise men, astrologers, magicians, or soothsayers of *Babylon* could find out, he goes to *Hananiah, Mishael*, and *Azariah*, his companions, and they *agree together* that they will *unitedly desire* the mercies of the God of heaven, concerning this secret; and their joint request was soon granted. God put great honor upon them, above all the wise men of *Babylon*, not only to their great joy, but also to the admiration and astonishment of *Nebuchadnezzar*; insomuch that the great and haughty monarch, as we are told, fell upon his face and worshiped *Daniel,* and owned that *his God was of a truth a God of gods,* and he greatly promoted *Daniel* and his praying companions in the province of *Babylon.*

Esther, when she had a yet more important request to make, for the saving of the church of God, and the whole *Jewish* nation, dispersed through the empire of *Persia,* when on the brink of ruin, sends to all the *Jews* in the city of *Shushan,* to pray and fast with her and her maidens; and their *united prayers* prevail; so that the event was wonderful. Instead of the intended destruction of the *Jews,* their enemies are destroyed everywhere, and they are defended, honored, and promoted; their sorrow and distress is turned into great gladness, feasting, and triumph, and mutual joyful congratulations.

The witness of our Lord Jesus Christ

The encouragement to explicit agreement in prayer is great from such instances as these; but it is yet greater from those wonderful words of our blessed Redeemer, "I say unto you, that if any two of you shall agree on earth, touching any thing that you shall ask, it shall be done for them of my Father which is in heaven" (Matt. 18:19). Christ is pleased to give this great encouragement to the union of his followers in this excellent and holy exercise of seeking and serving God; a holy union and communion of his people being that which he greatly desires and delights in; that which he came into the world to bring to pass; that which he especially prayed for with his dying breath (John 17:21), that which he died for; and which was one chief end of the whole affair of our redemption by him; "In whom we have redemption through his blood, the forgiveness of sins, according to the riches of his grace, wherein he hath abounded towards us in all wisdom and prudence; having made known to us the mystery of his will, according to his good pleasure, which he hath purposed in himself: that in the dispensation of the fullness of times, he might gather in one all things in Christ, both which are in heaven, and which are on earth, even in him" (Eph. 1:7–9).

STUDY QUESTIONS

1. It is important to make sure that we understand all that Edwards is calling for in this summons to prayer. Let us remember that he is urging *explicit agreement and visible union of God's people in extraordinary prayer.* Define in your own words the following terms:

   a. explicit agreement:
   b. visible union:
   c. extraordinary prayer:

2. Now, in one sentence, using the definitions you prepared above, describe what this would look like in your church. Imagine yourself talking to another person about the kind of prayer you are proposing. How would you say it?

3. But let's not lose sight of the focus: . . . *for the revival of religion and the advancement of Christ's kingdom on earth.* Based

on what we have read and discussed thus far, define the following:

a. revival of religion:

b. advancement of Christ's kingdom:

4. Imagine the friend you are talking to above asking, "But what's the purpose of such prayer? What are we trying to achieve?" Using the two definitions above, how would you respond?

5. Continue your prayers for revival using Psalms 67, 80, and 44. In the week to come, using your answers to the questions above, together with these psalms, recruit one more person to join you in a time of prayer according to what Edwards is teaching us. Begin meeting regularly with that person to pray for revival.

❧ *Part 3* ❧

OBJECTIONS ANSWERED

❧ *Chapter 7* ❧

SUCH PRAYER IS SUPERSTITIOUS, WHIMSICAL, OR LEGALISTIC

Edwards now turns to defend his proposal against what he imagines some objections to it will be. He contends that his proposal is not mere superstition, or whimsy, or Pharisaism, but a reasonable and effective way of helping Christians lay hold of the promise of Scripture.

❧

I come now, as was proposed, in the *third* place, to answer and obviate some objections, which some may be ready to make against what has been proposed.

THAT SUCH PRAYER IS SUPERSTITIOUS

Some may be ready to say that for Christians in such a manner to set apart *certain seasons*, every week, and every quarter, to be religiously observed and kept for the purposes proposed, from year to year, would be, in effect, to *establish* certain periodical times of *human* invention and appointment, to be *kept holy to God;* and so to do the very thing that has ever been objected against, by a very great part of the most eminent Christians and divines among protestants, as what men have no right to do; it being for them to *add* to God's institutions, and introduce their own inventions and establishments into the stated worship of God, and lay unwarrantable bonds on men's consciences, and do what naturally tends to *superstition.*

The proposal does not bind a person's conscience

To this I would say, there can be no justice in such an objection against this proposal. Indeed, that caution appears in the project itself, and in the manner in which it is proposed to us, that there is not so much as any color for that objection. The proposal is such, and so well guarded, that there seems to be no room for the weakest Christian who well observes it, to understand those things to be implied in it, which have indeed been objected against by many eminent Christians and divines among protestants, as entangling men's consciences, and adding to divine institutions, and so forth. Here is not pretense of establishing anything by *authority;* no appearance of any claim of *power* in the proposers,[1] or *right* to have any regard paid to their determinations or proposals, by virtue of any deference due to *them,* in any respect. So far from that, they ex-

---

1. He means those Scottish pastors whose *Memorial* Edwards is responding to, and which we have omitted. He is defending their proposal for prayer, and, indirectly, his own, in these remarks.

pressly propose what they have thought of to others, for their amendments and improvements, declaring that they choose rather to receive and spread the directions and proposals of others, than to be the first authors of any.

No new times for worship proposed

No times, not sanctified by God's own institution, are proposed to be observed more than others, under any notion of such times being, in any respect, more holy, or more honorable, or worthy of any preference, or distinguishing regard; either as being sanctified, or made honorable, by authority, or by any great events of divine providence, or any relation to any holy persons or things; but only as circumstantially convenient, helpful to memory, especially free from worldly business, near to the times of the administration of public ordinances, and so forth. None attempts to lay any bonds on others, with respect to this matter; or to desire that they should lay any bonds on themselves; or look on themselves as under any obligation, either by power or promise; or so much as come into any absolute determination in their own minds, to set apart any stated days from secular affairs; or even to fix on any part of such days, without liberty to alter circumstances, as shall be found expedient; and also liberty left to a future alteration of judgment, as to expediency, on future trial and consideration. All that is proposed is that such as fall in with what is proposed in their judgments and inclinations, while they do so should strengthen, assist, and encourage their brethren that are of the same mind, by visibly consenting and joining with them in the affair. Is here anything like making laws in matters of conscience and religion, or adding men's institutions to God's; or any show of imposition, or superstitious esteeming and preferring one day above another, or any possible ground of entanglement of anyone's conscience?

A *voluntary matter only*

For men to go about by *law* to establish and limit circumstances of worship, not established or limited by any law of God, such as precise time, place, and order, may be in many respects of dangerous tendency. But surely it cannot be unlawful or improper, for Christians to come into some agreement, with regard to these circumstances; for it is impossible to carry on any social worship without it. There is no institution of Scripture requiring any people to meet together to worship God in such a spot of ground, or at such an hour of the day; but yet these must be determined by agreement; or else there will be no social worship, in any place, or any hour.

So we are not determined by institution,[2] what the precise order of the different parts of worship shall be; what shall precede, and what shall follow; whether praying or singing shall be first, and what shall be next, and what shall conclude: but yet some order must be agreed on, by the congregation that unite in worship, in any way of method at all. If a congregation of Christians agree to begin their

2. He means explicit biblical instruction.

public worship with *prayer*, next to *sing*, then to attend on the *preaching* of the word, and to conclude with *prayer*; and do by consent carry on their worship in this order from year to year; though this order is not appointed in Scripture, none will call it *superstition*. And if a great number of congregations, through a whole land, or more lands than one, do, by a common consent, keep the same method of public worship; none will pretend to find fault with it.

But yet for any to go about to bind all to such a method, would be usurpation and imposition. And if such a precise order should be regarded as sacred, as though no other could be acceptable to God, this would be superstition. If a particular number of Christians shall agree that besides the stated public worship of the sabbath, they will, when their circumstances allow, meet together, to carry on some religious exercises, on a sabbath-day night, for their mutual edification; or if several societies agree to meet together in different places at that time; this is no superstition; though there be no institution for it. If people in different congregations, voluntarily agree to take turns to meet together in the house of God, to worship him and hear a public lecture, once a month, or once in six weeks; it is not unlawful though there be no institution for it: but yet, to do this as a thing sacred, indispensable, and binding men's consciences, would be superstition. If Christians of several neighboring congregations, instead of a lecture, agree on some special occasion to keep a *circular fast*, each congregation taking it by turn in a certain time and order, fixed on by consent; or if, instead of keeping fast by turns, on different days, one on one week and one on another, they shall all agree to keep a fast on the *same day,* and to do this either once or frequently, according as they shall judge their own circumstances, or the dispensations of divine providence, or the importance of the mercy they seek, require; is there any more superstition in this?

That Such Prayer Is Whimsical

Some may be ready to say, there seems to be something *whimsical* in its being insisted on that God's people in different places should put up their prayers for this mercy *at the same time;* as though their prayers would be more *forcible* on that account; and as if God would not be so likely to hear prayers offered up by many, though they happened not to pray at the same time, as he would if he heard them all at the same moment.

To this I would say, if such an objection be made, it must be through misunderstanding. It is not signified or implied in anything said in the proposal, or in any arguments made use of to enforce it that I have seen, that the prayers of a great number in different places, will be more forcible, merely because of that circumstance, of their being put up at the same time. It is indeed supposed that it will be very expedient that certain times for united prayer should be agreed on: which it may be, without implying the thing supposed in the objection, on the following accounts.

It is expedient to promote union in prayer

This seems to be a proper expedient for promoting and maintaining an *union* among Christians of distant places, in *extraordinary prayer for such a mercy.* It appears, from what was before observed, that there ought to be extraordinary prayers among Christians for this mercy; and that it is fit God's people should agree and unite in it. Though there be no reason to suppose that prayers will be more prevalent, merely from the circumstance that different persons pray exactly *at the same time;* yet there be more reason to hope that prayers for such mercy will be prevalent, when God's people are *very much in prayer* for it, and when many of them are *united* in it. If therefore agreeing on certain times for united and extraordinary prayer, be a likely means to promote an union of many in extraordinary prayer, then there is more reason to hope that there will be *prevalent* prayer for such a mercy, on occasion of certain times for extraordinary prayer being agreed on. But that agreeing on certain times for united extraordinary prayer, is a likely and proper means to promote and maintain such prayer, I think will be easily evident to anyone that considers the matter. If there should be only a loose agreement or consent to it as a duty, or a thing fit and proper that Christians should be much in prayer for the revival of religion, and much more in it than they used to be, without agreeing on particular times, how liable would such a lax agreement be to be soon forgotten, and that extraordinary prayerfulness, which is fixed to no certain times, to be totally forgotten!

To be sure, distant parts of the church of Christ would have no confidence in one another, that this would not be the case. If these ministers in *Scotland,* for instance, instead of the proposal they have made, had sent abroad only a general proposal that God's people should, for the time to come, be much in more prayer for the advancement of Christ's kingdom, than had been common among Christians heretofore; and they should hear their proposals were generally allowed to be good; and that ministers and people, in one place and another, owned that it was a very proper thing; could they, from this only, have the like grounds of dependence that God's people, in various parts of the Christian world, would indeed henceforward act unitedly, in maintaining extraordinary prayer for this mercy? And how much more promising would it be, if they should not only hear that the duty in general was approved of, but also that particular times were actually fixed on for the purpose, and an agreement and joint resolution was come into, that they would, unless extraordinarily hindered, set apart such particular seasons to be spent in this duty, from time to time, maintaining this practice for a certain number of years!

Union in prayer makes visibility possible

For God's people in distant places to agree on certain times for extraordinary prayer, wherein they will unitedly put up their requests to God, is a means fit and proper to be used, in order to the *visibility* of their union in such prayer.

Union among God's people in prayer is truly beautiful, as shown before; it is beautiful in the eyes of Christ, and it is justly beautiful and amiable in the eyes of Christians. And if so, then it must needs be desirable to Christians that such union should be visible. If it would be a lovely sight in the eyes of the church of Christ, and much to their comfort, to behold various and different parts of the church *united* in extraordinary prayer for the general outpouring of the Spirit, then it must be desirable to them that such an union should be *visible*, that they may behold it. But agreement and union of a multitude in their worship becomes visible, by an agreement in some external visible circumstances. Worship itself becomes visible worship, by something external and visible belonging to the worship, and no other way: therefore, union and agreement of many in worship becomes visible no other way, but by union and agreement in the external and visible acts and circumstances of worship.

Such union and agreement becomes visible, particularly by an agreement in those two visible circumstances, *time and place*. When a number of Christians live near together, and their number and situation is convenient, and they have a desire visibly to unite in any acts of worship, they are wont to make their union and agreement visible by an union in both these circumstances. But when a much greater number of Christians, dwelling in distant places so that they cannot unite by worshiping in the same place, yet desire a visible union in some extraordinary worship; they are wont to make their union and agreement visible, by agreeing only in the former of those circumstances, namely, that of *time*. This is common in the appointment of public fasts and thanksgivings; the *same day* is appointed, for the performance of that extraordinary worship, as a visible note of union. To this common sense leads Christians in all countries. And the wisdom of God seems to dictate the same thing in appointing that his people, in their stated and ordinary public worship every week, should manifest this union and communion one with another, as one holy society; by offering up their worship on the same day; for the greater glory of their common Lord, and the greater edification and comfort of the whole body.

Union in prayer greatly magnifies the name of Christ

If any yet find fault with the proposal of certain times to be agreed on by God's people in different places, in the manner set forth in the [proposal], I would ask whether they object against *any such thing,* as a visible agreement of God's people, in different parts of the world, in extraordinary prayer, for the coming of Christ's kingdom? Whether such a thing being visible, would not be much for the public honor of God's name? And whether it would not tend to Christians' assistance, and encouragement in the duty, and also to their mutual comfort, by a manifestation of that union which is amiable to Christ and Christians, and to promote a Christian union among professing Christians in general? And whether we have not reason to think from the word of God that before that great revival of religion foretold is accomplished, there will be a visible union of the people of God, in various parts of the world, in extra-ordinary prayer for this mercy?

If these things are allowed, I would then ask further, whether any method can be thought of or devised, whereby an express agreement, and visible union of God's people, in different parts of the world, can be maintained, but this, or some other equivalent to it? If there be any express agreement about any extraordinary prayer at all, it must first be proposed by some, and others must fall in, as represented in my text. And if extraordinary prayer be agreed on, and maintained by many in different places, visibly one to an-other, then it must be agreed with regard to some circum-stances, what extraordinary prayer shall be kept up; and this must be seen and heard of, from one to another. But how shall this be, when *no times* are agreed upon, and it is never known, by those in different parts, when, or how of-ten, any others do attend this extraordinary prayer? The consequence must necessarily be that it can never be known how far, or in what respect, others join with them in extra-ordinary prayer, or whether they do it at all; and not so much as one circumstance of extraordinary prayer will be *visible*; and indeed nothing will be visible about it. So that I think anybody that well considers the matter, will see that he who determines to oppose such a method as is proposed to us in the [proposal], and all others equivalent to it, is, in effect, determined to oppose there ever being any such thing at all, as an agreed and visibly united extraordinary prayer, in the church of God, for a general outpouring of the Spirit.

That such a union in prayer will affect the minds of men

Though it would not be reasonable to suppose that merely such a circumstance, as many people praying at the same time, will directly have any prevalence with God; yet such a circumstance may reasonably be supposed to have influence on the minds of *men*. Will any deny that it has any reasonable tendency to encourage, animate, or in any respect to help the mind of a Christian in serving God in any duty of religion, to join with a Christian congregation, and to see an assembly of his dear brethren around him, at the same time engaged with him in the same duty? And supposing one in this assembly of saints is blind, but has ground of satisfaction that there is present a multitude of God's people united with him in the same service; will any deny that his supposing this, and being satisfied of it, can have any reasonable influence upon his mind, to excite and encourage him, or in any respect to assist him in his worship? The encouragement that one has in worship, by others being united with him, is not merely by the external senses, but by the knowledge that mind has of that union, or the satisfaction the understanding has that others, at that time, have their minds engaged with him in the same service; which may be, when those unitedly engaged are at a distance one from another, as well as when they are present. If one be present in a worshiping assembly, and sees their external behavior; their *union* with him in worship, he does not see; and what he sees, encourages him in worship, only as an evidence of that union and concurrence which is out of sight. And a person may have such evidence of this, concerning *absent* worshipers, as may give him satisfaction of their union with him, no less than if they were present. And therefore the consideration of others being at the same time engaged with him in worship, though absent, may as reasonably animate and encourage him in his worship, as if they were present.

There is no wisdom in finding fault with human nature, as God has made it. Things that exist now, are in themselves no more important, than the like things, in time past, or in time to come: yet, it is evident that the consideration of things present, at least in most cases, especially affects human nature. For instance, if a man could be certainly informed that his dear child at a distance was now under some extreme suffering; or that an absent most dear friend was at this time thinking of him, and in the exercise of great affection toward him, or in the performance of some great deed of friendship; or, if a pious parent should know that now his child was in the act of some enormous wickedness; or that, on the contrary, he was now in some eminent exercise of grace, and in the performance of an extraordinary deed of virtue and piety; would not those things be more affecting to human nature, for being considered as things at the present time, than if considered as at some distance of time, either past or future? Hundreds of other instances might be mentioned wherein it is no less plain that the consideration of the present existence of things, gives them advantage to affect the minds of men. Yea, it is undoubtedly so with things in general that take any hold at all of our affections, and toward which we are not indifferent. And if the mind of a particular child of God is disposed to be affected by the consideration of the religion of other saints, and of their union and concurrence with him in any particular duty or act of religion, I can see no reason why the human mind should not be more moved by the object of its affection, when considered as present, as well in this case, as in any other case: yea, I think, we may on good grounds determine there is none.

Nor may we look upon it as an instance of the peculiar *weakness* of human nature, that men are more affected with things considered as *present,* than those that are distant: but it seems to be a thing common to finite minds, and so to all created intelligent beings. Thus, the angels in heaven have joy, on occasion of the conversion of a sinner, when recent, beyond what they have in that which has been long past. If any therefore shall call it silly and whimsical in any, to value and regard such a circumstance, in things of religion, as their existing at the present time, so as to be the more affected with them for that; they must call the host of angels in heaven a parcel of silly and whimsical beings.

I remember, the *Spectator* (whom none will call a whimsical author), somewhere speaking of different ways of dear friends mutually expressing their affection, and maintaining a kind of intercourse, in absence from one another, mentions such an instance as this, with much approbation: that two friends, who were greatly endeared one to another, when about to part, and to be for a considerable time necessarily absent, that they might have the comfort of the enjoyment of daily mutual expressions of friendship in their absence; agreed that they would, every day, precisely at such an hour, retire from all company and business, to pray for one another. Which agreement they so valued and so strictly observed that when the hour came, scarce anything would hinder them. And rather than miss this opportunity, they would suddenly break off conversation, and abruptly leave company they were engaged with. If this be a desirable and amiable way of intercourse of particular friends, is it not a desirable and amiable way of maintaining intercourse and fellowship between brethren in Christ Jesus, and the various members of the holy family of God, in different parts of the world, to come into an agreement that they will set apart certain times, which they will spend with one accord, in extraordinary prayer to their heavenly Father, for the advancement of the kingdom, and the glory of their common dear Lord and Savior, and for each other's prosperity and happiness, and the greatest good of all their fellow-creatures through the world?

That Such Prayer Is Legalistic

Some perhaps may suppose that it looks too much like *Pharisaism,* when persons engage in any such extraordinary religious exercises, beyond what is appointed by express institution, for them thus designedly to make it manifest abroad in the world, and so openly to distinguish themselves from others.

Such has never before been considered the case

But all open engagement in extraordinary exercises of religion, not expressly enjoined by institution, is not *Pharisaism,* nor has ever been so reputed in the Christian church. As when a particular church or congregation of Christians agree together to keep a day of fasting and prayer, on some special occasion; or when public days of fasting and thanksgiving are kept, through a Christian province or country: and though it be ordinarily the manner for the civil magistrate to lead in setting apart such days; yet that alters not the case: if it be Pharisaism in the society openly to agree in such extraordinary exercises of religion, it is not less Pharisaism, for the heads of the society leading in the affair. And if the civil magistrate was not of the society of Christians, nor concerned about their affairs; yet this would not render it the less suitable for Christians, on proper occasions, jointly, and visibly one to another, to engage in such extraordinary exercises of religion, and to keep days of fasting and thanksgiving by agreement.

The proposal is inclusive, not exclusive

It cannot be objected against what is proposed that it would look like affecting singularity, and open distinction from others in extraordinary religion, like the *Pharisees* of old: because it is evident the very design of the [proposal] is not to promote singularity and distinction, but as much as possible to avoid and prevent it. The end of the [proposal] is not to limit the thing proposed, that it may be practiced only by a few, in distinction from the generality; but on the contrary to make it as general among professing Christians as possible. Some had complied with the extraordinary duty proposed, and therein had been distinguished from others, for two years, before the *Memorial* was published; and they were more distinguished than they desired; and therefore sent abroad this *Memorial,* that the practice might be more spread, and become more general, that they might be less distinguished. What they evidently seek, is to bring to pass as general a compliance as possible of Christians of all denominations, *entreating that the desire of concurrence and assistance, contained in the* Memorial, *may by no means be understood as restricting to any particular denomination or party, or those who are of such or such opinions about any former instances of remarkable religious concern; but to be extended to all, who shall vouchsafe any attention to the proposal, and have at heart the interest of vital Christianity, and the power of godliness: and who, however differing about other things, are convinced of the importance of fervent prayer, to promote that common interest, and of Scripture persuasives, to promote such prayer.*

STUDY QUESTIONS

1. In this chapter, as he begins to respond to objections he can imagine against his proposal, Edwards begins to lay out a clearer picture of what he has in mind. Let's try to flesh out his proposal in words of our own. First, what does Edwards seem to have in mind concerning the time

or times for such prayer? When? With what kind of frequency? For how long shall we keep at it?

2. Whom does Edwards envision being involved in such prayer? How are they to be contracted for it? How could that be expedited?

3. What is to be the subject matter of these times of prayer? Or the objective? (You might want to review the questions to the last chapter.)

4. How can believers encourage one another to make time for this effort and to persevere in it? What are some ways they could learn about what's happening in the church in other parts of the world? Why would that be important in this effort?

5. Meet with your prayer partner to pray through Psalms 67, 80, and 44. Let the words of these psalms lead you to be very specific in what you pray for as you plead with the Lord to revive his church.

❊ Chapter 8 ❊

THE GREAT TRIBULATION MUST COME FIRST

In this section Edwards argues against the view that the church must go through a violent and general period of tribulation before its days of final glory appear.

Another objection, very likely to arise in the minds of many against such extraordinary prayer for the speedy coming of Christ's kingdom, is that we have *no reason to expect it,* till there first come a time of most extreme *calamity* to the church, and a prevalence of her *anti-Christian* enemies against her; even that which is represented in Revelation 11 by the *slaying of the witnesses;* but have reason to determine the contrary.

THE OBJECTION EXPLAINED

It is indeed an opinion that seems pretty much to have obtained, that before the fulfillment of the promises relating to the church's latter-day glory, there must come a most terrible time, a time of extreme suffering, and dreadful persecution of the church of Christ; wherein *Satan* and *antichrist* are to obtain their greatest victory over her, and she is to be brought lower than ever by her enemies. This opinion has chiefly arisen from the manner of interpreting and applying the fore-mentioned prophecy of the slaying of the witnesses; and must needs be a great hindrance, with regard to such an affair as is proposed to us in the *Memorial*. If persons expect no other, than that the more the glorious times of Christ's kingdom are hastened, the sooner will come this dreadful time, wherein the generality of God's people must suffer so extremely, and the church of Christ be almost extinguished, and blotted out from under heaven; how can it be otherwise than a great damp to their hope, their courage and activity, in praying for, and reaching after the speedy introduction of those glorious promised times?

As long as this opinion is retained, it will undoubtedly ever have this unhappy influence on the minds of those that wish well to *Zion*. It will tend to damp and keep down joyful expectation in prayer; and even in great measure to prevent all earnest, animated, and encouraged prayer, in God's people, for this mercy, at any time before it is actually fulfilled. For they who proceed on this hypothesis in their prayers, must, at the same time that they pray for this glorious day, naturally conclude within themselves, that they shall never live to see on earth any dawning of it, but only the dismal time that shall precede it; in which the far greater part of God's people who shall live till then, shall die under the extreme cruelties of their persecutors. And the more they expect that God will answer their prayers, by speedily bringing on the promised glorious day, the more must they expect themselves to have a share in those dreadful things that nature shrinks at, and also expect to see what a renewed nature dreads; even the prevailing of God's enemies, and the almost total extinction of true religion in the world. And on this *hypothesis,* these discouragements are like to attend the prayers of God's people, till that dismal time be actually come; and when that is come, those who had been prophesying and praying in sackcloth, shall generally be slain: and after that time is over, then the glorious day shall immediately commence. So that this notion tends to discourage all earnest prayer in the church of God for that glorious coming of Christ's kingdom, till it be actually come; and that is to hinder its ever being at all.

This opinion being of such hurtful tendency, it is a thousand pities it should be retained, if truly there be no good ground for it. Therefore in answer to this objection, I would, with all humility and modesty, examine the foundation of that opinion, of such a dreadful time of victory of antichrist over the church, yet to be expected: and particularly shall endeavor to show that the *slaying of the witnesses,* foretold [in] Revelation 11:7–10, is not an event that yet remains to be fulfilled. To this end I would propose the following things to consideration.

THE PROPHECY CLARIFIED[1]

The time wherein the *witnesses lie dead in the streets of the great city,* doubtless, signifies the time wherein the true church of Christ is lowest of all, most of all prevailed against by antichrist, and nearest to an utter extinction; the time wherein there is left the least visibility of the church of Christ yet subsisting in the world, least remains of anything appertaining to true religion, whence a revival of it can be expected, and wherein all means of it are most abolished, and the state of the church is in all respects furthest from any hopes of its ever flourishing again. For before this, the witnesses *prophesy in sackcloth;* but now they are *dead:* before this, they were kept low indeed, yet there was life, and power to bring plagues on their enemies, and so much of true religion left, as to be a continual torment to them. They have now entirely extirpated them, are completely delivered from them, and from all that might give them any fear of being troubled with them any more.

This time, wherever it is fixed, doubtless, is the time, not only wherein fewest professors of the true religion are

---

1. Edwards's point in this section seems to be that such a period of great persecution, when true religion has all but disappeared, seems most unlikely, given the state of Christianity in the world at present. It does not seem possible that such a time will come that will exceed such times as have already been, or that the Protestant religion—and even the Catholic faith—will be rolled back to such a state. It would take a miracle, like the flood, to accomplish such a thing. Therefore, he implies, the period referenced in this prophecy must already have come.

left in the world; but a time wherein the truth shall be farthest out of sight, and out of reach, and most forgotten;
wherein there are left fewest beams of light, or traces of
truth, fewest means of information, and opportunities of
coming to the knowledge of the truth; and so a time of the
most barbarous ignorance, most destitute of all history,
monuments, and memory of things appertaining to true religion, or things the knowledge of which hath any tendency
to bring truth again to light; and most destitute of learning, study, and inquiry.

Now, if we consider the present state of mankind, is it
credible that a time will yet come, exceeding, in these respects, all times before the Reformation? And that such a
time will come before the fall of antichrist, unless we set
that at a much greater distance, than the farthest that any
have yet supposed? It is next to impossible that such a
change should be brought about in so short a time: it cannot be without a miracle. In order to it, not only must the
popish[2] nations so prevail, as utterly to extirpate the
protestant religion through the earth; but must do many
other things, far more impossible for them to effect, in order to cover the world with so gross and confirmed a dark-

2. Like many Reformed believers of his day, following the original version of the *Westminster Confession of Faith,* Edwards seems to have
regarded the pope as antichrist and Roman Catholicism as the false
prophet of Revelation. The *Confession* has since been amended to
delete all such language, and most Reformed communions no longer
regard the pope or the Catholic Church in this way.

ness, and to bury all light and truth in so deep an oblivion, and so far out of all means and hopes of revival. And not only must a vast change be made in the *protestant* world, but the *popish* nations must be strangely metamorphosed; and they themselves must be terribly persecuted by some other power, in order to bring them to such a change: nor would persecution without extirpation be sufficient for it. If there should be another universal deluge, it might be sufficient to bring things to such a pass; provided a few ignorant barbarous persons only were preserved in an ark: and it would require some catastrophe not much short of this to effect it.

THE FALL OF ANTICHRIST

At the *Reformation*,[3] in the days of *Luther, Calvin,* and others their contemporaries, the threatened destruction of antichrist, the dreadful enemy that had long oppressed and worn out the saints, was *begun.* Nor was it a small beginning; for antichrist hath fallen, at least half-way to the ground, from that height of power and grandeur he was in before. Then began the vials of God's wrath to be *poured out on the throne of the beast,* to the great shaking of its foundations, and diminution of its extent; so that the *pope* lost near half of his former dominions: and as to the degree of

3. The Protestant Reformation, 1517–1648, which saw the rise of Protestantism and the reform of many abuses in the Roman Catholic Church.

authority and influence over what is left, he is not possessed of what he had before. God now at length, in answer to the long-continued cries of his people, awakened as one out of sleep, and began to deliver his church from her exceeding low state, under the great oppression of this grand enemy, and to restore her from her exile and bondage in the spiritual *Babylon*[4] and *Egypt*. It is not agreeable to the analogy of God's dispensations that after this he should desert his people, hide himself from them even more than before, leave them more than ever in the hands of their enemy; and is it credible that all this advantage of the church against antichrist should be entirely given up and lost, his power and tyranny be more confirmed, the church more entirely subdued than ever before, and further from all help and means of recovery? This is not God's way of dealing with his people, or with their enemies. His work of salvation is perfect: when he has begun such a work he will carry it on: when he once causes the day of deliverance to dawn to his people, after such a long night of dismal darkness, he will not extinguish the light, and cause them to return again to midnight darkness. When he has begun to enkindle the blessed fire, he will not quench the smoking flax, till he hath brought forth judgment unto victory. When once the church, after her long and sore travail, has brought forth her man-child, and wrought some deliverance, her enemies

4. Edwards may well have in mind Luther's revolutionary tract of 1520, *The Pagan Servitude of the Church*, or, as it is popularly known, *The Babylonian Captivity of the Church*.

shall never be able to destroy this child, though an infant; but it shall ascend up to heaven, and be set on high out of their reach.

EXAMPLES FROM THE HISTORY OF THE JEWISH CHURCH

The destruction that God often foretold and threatened to ancient *Babylon* (which is often referred to in the revelation, as a great type of the anti-Christian church) was gradually accomplished, by various steps at a great distance of time one from another. It was begun in the conquest of *Cyrus;*[5] and was further accomplished by *Darius,* about *eighteen* years after, by a yet greater destruction, wherein it was brought much nearer to utter desolation; but it was about *two hundred and twenty-three* years after this, before the ruin of it was perfected, and the prophecies against full accomplished, in its being made an utter and perpetual desolation, without any human inhabitant, becoming the dwelling-place for owls, dragons, and other doleful creatures.

But yet when God had once begun to destroy her, he went on till he finished, and never suffered her any more to recover and establish her former empire. So the restitution of the Jewish church, after the Babylonish captivity, was by various steps; there were several times of return of the Jews

5. Founder and ruler of the Persian dynasty (559–530 B.C.) that supplanted ancient Babylon.

from captivity, and several distinct decrees of the Persian emperors, for restoring and rebuilding Jerusalem, and re-establishing the Jewish church and state. It was also done in turbulent times; there were great interruptions, checks, and violent oppositions, and times wherein the enemy did much prevail. But yet when God had once begun the work, he also made an end; he never suffered the enemies of the Jews to bring Jerusalem to such a state of desolation as it had been in before, till the promised restoration was complete. Again, the deliverance of God's church from the oppression of *Antiochus Epiphanes*[6] (another known type of antichrist), was gradual; they were first assisted a little by the Maccabees;[7] afterwards, the promised deliverance was completed in the recovery of Jerusalem, the restoration of the temple, the miserable end of Antiochus, and the consequent more full deliverance of the whole land. But after God once began to appear for the help of his church in that instance, though it had seemed dead and past all hope, he never suffered Antiochus to prevail to that degree again. The utmost strength of this great monarch was used, from time to time, to order it, and his vast empire was engaged against a handful that opposed them; yet God never forsook the work of his own hands; when he had begun to deliver his people, he also made an end.

6. Greek king who, during the period following the close of the Old Testament, sought to Hellenize Jewish culture and desecrated the temple of the Jews.
7. Leaders of a Jewish rebellion against Antiochus Epiphanes.

And so Haman, that proud and inveterate enemy of the Jews, who thought to extirpate the whole nation (who was also probably another type of antichrist), when he began to fall before Esther and Mordecai, never stayed, till his ruin and the church's deliverance were complete; Haman's wife speaks of it as an argument of his approaching inevitable full destruction, that he "had begun to fall" (Esther 6:13).

THE VISIBLE CHURCH INCREASING

If *anti-Christian* tyranny and darkness should hereafter so prevail against the protestant church—the true religion[8] and everything appertaining to it—as to bring things to the pass fore-mentioned, this would not so properly *answer the prophesy* of slaying the *two* witnesses; for doubtless, one reason why they are called *two witnesses,* is that the number of witnesses for the truth was (though sufficient yet) *very small.* This was remarkably the case in the dark times of popery; but since the Reformation, the number of those appearing on the side of true religion has not been so small. The visible church of Christ has been vastly large, in comparison with what it was before. The number of protestants has sometimes been thought nearly equal to that of the papists; and, doubtless, the number of true saints has been far greater than before.

8. It is a measure of how much things have changed in Protestantism since Edwards's day that no Protestant theologian would make this equation.

ANTICHRIST SHALL NO MORE
PREVAIL

It seems to be signified in prophecy that after the Reformation *antichrist* should *never* prevail against the church of Christ any more, as he had done before. I cannot but think that whoever reads and well considers what the learned Mr. Lowman has written on the five first vials (Rev. 16) in his late exposition on the *Revelation,* must think it to be very manifest that what is said (Rev. 16:10) of the pouring out of the fifth vial *on the throne of the beast* (for so it is in the original), is a prophecy of the Reformation. Then the vial of God's wrath was poured out on the throne of the beast, i.e., according to the language of Scripture, on his authority and dominion, greatly to weaken and diminish it, both in extent and degree. But when this is represented in prophecy, then it is added, "and his kingdom was full of darkness, and they gnawed their tongues for pain." If we consider what is commonly intended by similar phrases in the Scripture, I think we shall be naturally, and as it were necessarily, led to understand these words thus: their *policy,* by which heretofore they have prevailed, shall now fail them; their *authority* shall be weakened, their *dominion* greatly diminished, and all their *subtlety* shall not avail them to support the throne of the beast, or even again to extend his authority so far as it had been before extended, and to recover what is lost. All their crafty devices to this end shall be attended with vexatious, tormenting disappointment; they who have the management of the beast's kingdom, shall henceforward grope as in the dark, and stumble, and be confounded in their purposes, plots, and enterprises. Formerly their policy was greatly successful, as a light to guide them to their ends; but now their kingdom shall be full of darkness, and their wisdom shall fail them in all their devices to subdue the church of God.

The Scripture takes notice of the great policy and subtlety of the powers that support this kingdom: "And behold, in this horn were eyes like the eyes of a man" (Dan. 7:8). So it is said of *Antiochus Epiphanes,* that great type of antichrist: "A king of fierce countenance, and understanding dark sentences, shall stand up" (Dan. 8:23). "And through his policy also, shall he cause craft to prosper in his hand" (Dan. 8:25). This understanding and policy is the light of this kingdom, as true wisdom is the light of the spiritual *Jerusalem;* and therefore, when the light fails, then may the kingdom of this spiritual *Egypt* be said to be full of darkness. God henceforward will defend his people from these mystical *Egyptians,* as he defended *Israel* of old from *Pharaoh* and his host, when pursuing after them, by placing a cloud and darkness in their way, and so not suffering them to come nigh.

He will protect his church from the men of *that city that is spiritually called* Sodom, as *Lot's* house, wherein were the angels, was defended from the men of *Sodom,* by their being smitten with darkness or blindness, so that they wearied themselves to find the door; and as God defended the city in which was *Elisha,* the prophet and witness of the Lord, from the *Syrians,* when they compassed it about with horses and chariots, and a great host, to apprehend him, by smiting them with blindness. The Scripture teaches us that God is wont in this way to defend his church and people from their crafty and powerful enemies: "To set up on high those that be low, that those which mourn may be exalted to safety: he disappointeth the devices of the crafty, so that their hands cannot perform their enterprise: he taketh the wise in their own craftiness, and the counsel of the froward is carried headlong: they met with darkness in the daytime, and grope in the noon-day as in the night; but he saveth the poor from the sword, from their mouth, and from the hand of the mighty" (Job 5:11, etc.; see also Ps. 35:4, 6). On account of such defense of God's protestant church, with the disappointment and confusion of all the subtle devices, deep-laid schemes, and furious attempts of their *anti-Christian* enemies, to root them out, while they see them still maintaining their ground, in spite of all they do, it makes them as it were gnash their teeth, and bite their tongues for mere rage and vexation; agreeably to Psalm 123:[3], 9–10: "His righteousness endureth forever. . . . his horn shall be exalted with honor: the wicked shall see it and be grieved, and gnash with his teeth and melt away: the desire of the wicked shall perish."

Hitherto this prophecy has been very signally fulfilled; since the Reformation, the kingdom of antichrist has been remarkably filled with darkness in this respect. Innumerable have been the crafty devices and great attempts of the church of *Rome*, wherein they have exerted their utmost policy and power, to recover their lost dominions, and again to subjugate the protestant nations—the *northern heresy,* as they call it. They have wearied themselves in these endeavors for more than *two hundred* years past; but have hitherto been disappointed, and have often been strangely confounded. When their matters seemed to be brought to a degree of ripeness, and they triumphed as though their point was gained, their joy and triumph as suddenly turned into vexation and torment. How many have been their politic and powerful attempts against the protestant interest in our nation, in particular! And how wonderfully has God disappointed them from time to time! And as God has hitherto so remarkably fulfilled his word in defending his protestant church from antichrist, so I think we have ground to trust in him that he will defend it to the end.

THIS OBJECTION CREATES INCONSISTENCIES

The *hypothesis* of those who suppose that the slaying of the witnesses yet remains to be fulfilled, makes the prophecies of the *Revelation* to be *inconsistent* one with another. According to their *hypothesis,* that battle wherein the beast makes war with the witnesses, overcomes, and kills them, is the last and greatest conflict between antichrist and the church of Christ, which is to precede the utter overthrow of the *anti-Christian* kingdom (Rev. 11:7). And they must suppose so; for they suppose that immediately after the sufferings the church shall endure in that war, she shall arise, and as it were ascend into heaven; i.e., as they interpret it, the church shall be directly advanced to her latter-day rest, prosperity, and glory. And consequently, this conflict must be the same with that great battle between antichrist and the church, described in Revelation 16:13, to the end, and more largely Revelation 19:11, to the end. For that which is described in these places, is most indisputably the greatest and last conflict between the church and her *anti-Christian* enemies; on which the utter downfall of antichrist, and the church's advancement to her latter-day glory, shall be immediately consequent. And so the earthquake that attends the resurrection of the witnesses, Revelation 11:13, must be the same with that great earthquake described, Revelation 16:18. And the falling of the tenth part of the city must be the same with that terrible and utter destruction of antichrist's kingdom, Revelation 16:17, to the end.

But these things cannot be. The battle, Revelation 11:7, cannot be the same with that last and great battle between the church and antichrist, described [in] Revelation 16 and Revelation 19. For the things that are said of the one and the other, and their issue, are in no wise consistent. In that battle, Revelation 11, the church of God conflicts with her enemies in sorrow, sackcloth, and blood: but in the other the matter is represented exceedingly otherwise; the church goes forth to fight with antichrist, not in sackcloth and blood, but clothed in white raiment, Christ himself before them, as their captain, going forth in great pomp and magnificence, upon a "white horse, and on his head many crowns, and on his vesture and on his thigh a name written, *King of kings and Lord of lords."* And the saints who follow so glorious a leader to this great battle, follow him on "white horses, clothed in fine linen, white and clean," in garments of strength, joy, glory, and triumph; in the same kind of raiment that the saints appear in, when they are represented as triumphing with Christ, with palms in their hands (Rev. 7:9). And the issue of the latter of these conflicts is quite the reverse of the former. In the battle, "the beast makes war with the witnesses, and *overcomes them, and kills them"* (Rev. 11:7): the same is foretold, "I beheld, and the same horn made war with the saints, and prevailed against them" (Dan. 7:21). "And it was given unto him to make war with the saints, and to overcome them" (Rev. 12:7). But in the issue of the last and great battle, which the church shall have with her *anti-Christian* enemies, the church shall OVERCOME THEM, AND KILL THEM: "These shall make war with the Lamb, and the Lamb shall overcome them; for he is Lord of lords, and King of kings; and they that are with him, are called, and chosen, and faithful" (Rev. 17:14).

In the conflict that the beast shall have with the witnesses, the "beast kills them, and their dead bodies lie unburied"; as though they were to be meat for the beasts of the earth, and fowls of heaven: but in the last battle, it is represented that Christ and his church "shall slay their enemies, and give their dead bodies to be meat for the fowls of heaven" (Rev. 19:17, etc.). There is no appearance, in the descriptions given of that last great battle, of any advantages gained in it by the enemies of the church, before they themselves are overcome; but all appearance of the contrary. The descriptions in the sixteenth and nineteenth chapters of the *Revelation* will by no means allow of such an advantage, as overcoming God's people, and slaying them; their lying dead for some time, and unburied, that their dead bodies may be for their enemies to abuse, trample on, and make sport with. In Revelation 16 we read of their being gathered together against the church, a mighty host, into the place called *Armageddon;* and then the first thing we hear of, is, the pouring out of the seventh vial of God's wrath, and a voice saying, "It is done." And so in the nineteenth chapter we have an account of the "beast, and the kings of the earth, and their armies, being gathered together to make war against him that sat on the horse, and against his army." And then the next thing we hear of, is that the "beast is taken, and with him the false prophet; *and that* these are both cast alive into the lake of fire; *and that* the remnant of their vast army are slain, and all the fowls filled with their flesh." The issue of the conflict of the beast with the witnesses, in the triumph of the church's enemies over God's people, looking on them as entirely vanquished, and their interest utterly ruined, past all recovery; "they that dwell on the earth shall see the dead bodies of the saints lying in the streets of the great city, and shall rejoice over them and make merry, and send gifts to one another." But the issue of that great and last battle is quite the reverse; it is the church's triumph over her enemies, as being utterly and forever destroyed.

Upon the whole I think there appears to be no reason from the prophecy concerning the *two witnesses* (Rev. 11) to expect any such general and terrible *destruction* of the church of Christ, before the utter downfall of *antichrist,* as some have supposed; but good reason to determine the contrary. It is true, there is abundant evidence in Scripture that there is yet remaining a *mighty conflict* between the church and her enemies—the most violent struggle of *Satan* and his adherents in opposition to true religion, and the most general commotion that ever was in the world, since the foundation of it to that time—and many particular Christians may suffer hard things in this conflict. But in the general, *Satan* and *antichrist* shall not get the victory, nor greatly prevail; on the contrary, they shall be entirely conquered, and utterly overthrown, in this great battle. So that I hope this prophecy of the *slaying of the witnesses,* will not stand in the way of a compliance with the proposal made to us, as a prevalent objection and discouragement.

STUDY QUESTIONS

1. Edwards's argument probably seems strange to us, but it has some points we need to compare with the rest of Scripture before we determine its worth. His basic point is that once God has begun his great work of creating and prospering his church, he will not allow anything to thwart its full realization. How does this view compare, for example, with a prophesy such as Daniel 2:44–45?

2. Edwards also wants to insist that the days of violent suppression of the faith are behind us; and, while Christians will continue to suffer for what they believe, yet true faith will increase on the earth, in spite of attempts to keep that from happening. Do you see any evidence in our day that these things are happening, just as Edwards believed?

3. And so he does not want us to be reluctant to pray for revival in the belief that this will hasten some day of great persecution. Persecution will happen, although not on a worldwide scale like it has in the past. Rather, he insists, we should pray for the continuing and accelerated unfolding of Christ's kingdom. Look at Psalm 85, another revival psalm. In what ways does this psalm seem to support Edwards's view (cf. vv. 8–9, 12–13)?

4. Take some time now to pray through Psalm 85, doing your best to make these words your own as you seek reviving grace from the Lord.

5. Review the goals you set for this study. Are you making any progress toward realizing them? In what ways?

❧ Chapter 9 ❧

THE FALL OF ANTICHRIST
MUST BE FAR OFF (1)

*Edwards begins a series of responses to a contemporary writer who had
made the claim that the fall of antichrist and the coming of the kingdom were yet many years off. He is persuaded that such a view is in-
correct, and he is worried that it will discourage prayer such as he is
proposing. Hence, he mounts a comprehensive effort to rebut this view.*

❧

A very learned and ingenious expositor of the *Revelation,*
Mr. Lowman, sets the fall of *antichrist,* and consequently the
coming of Christ's kingdom, at a *great distance;* supposing that
the *twelve hundred and sixty* years of antichrist's reign did not
begin till the year *seven hundred and fifty-six;* and consequently,
that it will not end till after the year *two thousand;* and this
opinion he confirms by a great variety of arguments.

IMPLICATIONS OF THIS OPINION

If this objection be allowed to be valid, and that
which ought to determine persons in an affair of this na-

ture, in connection with the duty before proved,[1] then the following things must be supposed, namely, that it is the will of God his people be much in prayer for this event; and particularly, that a little before its accomplishment his people be earnestly seeking, and importunately crying to God for it; but yet that it was God's design, before this time of extraordinary prayer and importunity, his church should understand precisely when the appointed time should be; and that accordingly he has now actually brought the fixed time to light, by means of Mr. Lowman.

But is it reasonable to suppose that this should be God's manner of dealing with his church; first to make known to them the precise time which he has unalterably fixed for showing his mercy to *Zion,* and then make it the duty of his church, in an extraordinary manner, to be by prayer inquiring of him concerning it, and saying, "How long, Lord!" that he would come quickly, hide himself no longer, have mercy upon *Zion,* awake as one out of sleep, openly manifest himself, and make bare his holy arm for the salvation of his people? That "they who make mention of the Lord should not keep silence, nor give him any rest, till he establish and make *Jerusalem* a praise in the earth"? And that the church should then say to Christ, "Make haste, my beloved, and be thou like a roe or a young hart on the mountain of spices"?

1. That is, that God calls his people to unite in prayer for revival for the coming of the Spirit and greater advancement of the kingdom.

"IT IS NOT FOR YOU TO KNOW ..."

It may be many ways for the comfort and benefit of God's church in her afflicted state, to know that the reign of antichrist is to be no more than one thousand two hundred and sixty years; and some things in general may be argued concerning the approach of it, when it is near: as the *Jews* could argue the approach of Christ's first coming, from *Daniel's* prophecy of the seventy weeks, though they knew not precisely when that seventy weeks would end.

The testimony of Christ

But it is not reasonable to expect that God should make known to us beforehand the *precise* time of Christ's coming in his kingdom. The disciples desired to know this, and manifested their desire to their Lord; but he told them plainly that "it was not for them to know the times and seasons, which the Father hath put in his own power" (Acts 1:6–7); and there is no reason to think it is any more for us than for them; or for Christ's disciples in these days any more than for his apostles in those days. God makes it the duty of his church to be importunately praying for it, and praying that it may come *speedily*; and not only to be praying for it, but to be seeking for it, in the use of proper means; endeavoring that religion may now revive everywhere, and *Satan's* kingdom be overthrown; and always to be waiting for it, being in a constant preparation for it, as servants that wait for the coming of their Lord, or virgins for the coming of the bridegroom, not knowing at what hour he will come. But God's making known beforehand the precise time of his coming, does not well consist with these things.

It is the revealed will of God that he should be inquired of by his people, by extraordinary prayer, concerning this great mercy, to do it for them, before it be fulfilled. And if any suppose that it is now found out precisely when the time is to be, and (the time being at a considerable distance) that now is not a proper season to begin this extraordinary prayer, I would, on this supposition, ask, When shall we begin? How long before the fixed and known time of the bestowment of this mercy comes, shall we begin to cry earnestly to God that this mercy may come, and that Christ would make haste like a roe, and so forth? For us to delay, supposing that we know the time to be far off, is not agreeable to the language of God's people in my text, "Come, let us go *speedily,* and pray before the Lord, and seek the Lord of hosts."

The testimony of Daniel

I acknowledge Mr. Lowman's exposition of the *Revelation* is, on many accounts, excellently written, giving great light into some parts of that prophecy; and especially his interpretation of the five first vials; yet his opinion with respect to the *time, times,* and *half* a time of antichrist's reign, is the less to be regarded, because it is expressly declared it should be sealed up and hid, and not known till *the time of the end* of this period. *Daniel,* in the last chapter of his prophecy, gives us an account, how the angel told him of a future time of great trouble and affliction to the church of

God, and then said to him, "But thou, O Daniel, *shut up the words, and seal the book, even to the time of the end*" (Dan. 12:4). And then the prophet proceeds to give an account of a vision he had of one earnestly inquiring of the angel of the Lord *how long it would be to the end* of this remarkable time of the church's trouble, saying, "How long shall it be to the end of these wonders?" (Dan. 12:5–6). The answer was, that "it should be for a time, times, and an half," and that when so long a time was past, then this wonderful affliction and scattering of the holy people should be finished (Dan. 12:7). But then *Daniel* tells us, in the next verse, that "he heard, but he understood not," and said, "O, my Lord, what shall be the end of these things?" He did not understand that general and mystical answer, that those things should have an end at the end of "a time, times, and an half"; he did not know by it, when this period would have an end: and therefore he inquires more particularly what the time of the end was. But the angel replies, "Go thy way, Daniel, the words are closed and sealed up, till the time of the end" (Dan. 12:9). I do not know what would have been more express. The angel gently rebukes this over-inquisitiveness of *Daniel,* very much as Christ did a like inquisitiveness of the disciples concerning the same matter, when he said to them, "It is not for you to know the times and seasons, that the Father hath put in his own power."

I think there can be no doubt but that this space of the church's great trouble, about the end of which *Daniel* inquires, is the same as that spoken of, Daniel 7:25 and Revelation 12:14, as the time of antichrist's reign, and the church's being in the wilderness; and not merely the time of the church's troubles by *Anitochus Epiphanes*. But we see, when *Daniel* has a mind to know particularly when this time would come to an end, he is bid to go away, and rest contented in ignorance of this matter: for, says the man clothed in linen, *the words are closed up, and sealed, till the time of the end*. That is, very plainly, the matter that you inquire about, shall not be known, but kept a great secret, till the time of the end actually comes, and all attempts to find it out before shall be in vain. And therefore when a particular divine appears, who thinks he has found it out, and has unsealed this matter, we may well think he is mistaken.

THAT THE FALL OF ANTICHRIST MAY BE MUCH NEARER

Though it is not for us to know the precise time of the fall of antichrist, yet I humbly conceive that we have no reason to suppose the event principally intended in the prophecies of antichrist's destruction to be at so great a *distance*, as Mr. Lowman places it; but have reason to think it to be much nearer. Not that I would set up myself as a person of equal judgment with Mr. Lowman in matters of this nature. As he differs from most other approved expositors of the *Apocalypse* in this matter; so I hope it will not appear vanity and presumption in me to differ from this particular expositor, and to agree with the greater number. And since his opinion stands so much in the way of that great and important affair, to promote which is the very end of this whole discourse,[2] I hope it will not look as though I affected to appear considerable among the interpreters of prophecy, and as a person of skill in these mysterious matters, when I offer some reasons against Mr. Lowman's opinion. It is surely great pity that it should be received as a thing clear and abundantly confirmed that the glorious day of antichrist's fall is at so great a distance, so directly tending to discourage all earnest endeavors after its speedy accomplishment, unless there be good and plain ground for it. I would therefore offer some things to consideration, which I think may justly make us look upon the opinion of this learned interpreter not so indubitable, as to hinder our prayer and hoping for its being fulfilled much sooner.

Objections to the Objection

The period of antichrist's reign, as this author has fixed it, seems to be the main point insisted on in his exposition of the Revelation; which he supposes a great many things in the scheme of prophecies delivered in that book concur to establish. But there are several things in that scheme which appear to me justly liable to exception.

Historical objections

Whereas it is represented that there are seven different successive heads of the beast; that five were past, and an-

2. He means prayer for revival.

other was to come, and to continue a short space, that might on some accounts be reckoned a seventh; and that antichrist was to follow next after this, as the eighth; but yet the foregoing not being properly one of the heads of the beast, he[3] was properly the seventh (Rev. 17:10–11). Mr. Lowman does not think with others that by the seventh that was to continue a short space, which would not be properly one of the heads of the beast, is meant *Constantine,* and the other Christian emperors; for he thinks they are reckoned as properly belonging to the sixth head of the beast; but that hereby is intended the government of Rome under the Gothic princes, and the exarchate of Ravenna, after the imperial form of government in Rome ceased in Augustulus, till the pope was invested with his temporal dominion, called St. Peter's patrimony, by Pepin, king of France, in the year 756. And he supposes that the wounding of one of the heads of the beast with a sword of death (Rev. 13:3–14) was not fulfilled in the destruction of the heathen empire, and the giving of the imperial power unto Christians, but in the destruction of the imperial form of government by the sword of the Goths, in the time of Augustulus.

But it seems to me to be very unlikely, that the Spirit of God should reckon *Constantine* and the Christian emperors as proper members, and belonging to one of the heads of that monstrous wild and cruel beast, compared to a leopard, a bear, and a devouring lion, that had a mouth speaking great things and blasphemies, and that rules by the power

3. Antichrist.

and authority of the dragon, or the devil; which beast is represented in this seventeenth chapter, as full of names of blasphemy, and of a bloody color, denoting his cruelty in persecuting the Christian church. For *Constantine,* instead of this, was a member of the Christian church, set by God in the most eminent station in his church; and was honored, above all other princes that ever had been in the world, as the great protector of his church, and her deliverer from the persecuting power of that cruel scarlet-colored beast. Mr. Lowman himself styles him *a Christian prince, and protector of the Christian religion.* God is very careful not to reckon his own people among the Gentiles, the visible subjects of *Satan:* "The people shall not be reckoned among the nations" (Num. 23:9). If they happen to be among them, he will be careful to set a mark upon them, as a note of distinction (Rev. 7:3, etc.); when God is reckoning up his own people, he leaves out those that have been noted for idolatry. As among the tribes that were sealed (Rev. 8), those idolatrous tribes of Ephraim and Dan are left out, and in the genealogy of Christ (Matt. 1), those princes that were chiefly noted for idolatry are left out. Much more would God be careful not to reckon his own people, especially such Christian princes as have been the most eminent instruments of overthrowing idolatry, amongst idolaters: and as members and heads of that kingdom that is noted in Scripture as the most notorious and infamous of all, for abominable idolatry, opposition, and cruelty to the true worshipers of God. And especially not to reckon them as properly belonging to one of those seven heads of this monarchy, of which very heads it is particularly noted that they had on them the names of *blasphemy* (Rev. 13:1), which Mr. Lowman himself supposes to signify *idolatry*.

Therefore, Constantine not part of the beast

It was therefore worthy of God, agreeable to his manner, and might well be expected that when he was reckoning up the several successive heads of this beast, and *Constantine* and his successors came in the way, and there was occasion to mention them, to set a mark, or note of distinction, on them, signifying that they did not properly belong to the beast, nor were to be reckoned as belonging to the heads; and therefore are to be skipped over in the reckoning; and antichrist, though the eighth head of the Roman empire, is to be reckoned the seventh head of the beast. This appears to me abundantly the most just and natural interpretation of Revelation 17:10–11. It is reasonable to suppose that God would take care to make such a note in this prophetical description of this dreadful beast, and not by any means to reckon *Constantine* as belonging properly to him. If we reckon *Constantine* as a member of this beast having seven heads and ten horns, described in Revelation 17, and as properly one of his heads, then he was also properly a member of the great red dragon with seven heads and ten horns that warred with the woman (Rev. 12). For the seven heads and ten horns of that dragon are plainly the same with the seven heads and ten horns of the beast. So that this makes *Constantine* a visible member of the devil; for we are told expressly of that dragon that he was *that old serpent, called the devil and Satan* (Rev. 12:9).

And to suppose that *Constantine* is reckoned as belonging to one of the heads of that dragon, is to make these prophecies inconsistent with themselves. For in the twelfth chapter, we have represented a war between the dragon and the woman clothed with the sun; which woman, as all agree, is the church; but *Constantine,* as all do also agree, belonged to the woman, was a member of the Christian church, and was on that side in the war against the dragon; yea, was the main instrument of that great victory obtained over the dragon (Rev. 12:9–12). What an inconsistency therefore is it, to suppose that he was at the same time a member and head of that very dragon which fought with the woman, and yet which *Constantine* himself fought with, overcame, and gloriously triumphed over! It is not therefore to be wondered at that God was careful to distinguish *Constantine* from the proper heads of the beast: it would have been a wonder if he had not. God seems to have been careful to *distinguish* him, not only in his word, but in his *providence,* by so ordering it that this Christian emperor should be removed from Rome, the city which God had given up to the seat of the power of the beast and of its heads, and that he should have the seat of his empire elsewhere.

STUDY QUESTIONS

1. Let's try to keep this chapter in perspective. Edwards is responding to a claim made by a certain writer that the fall of antichrist will be yet many years off (although, perhaps, not so many more!). If so, then what does this do to the

many exhortations of Scripture to pray urgently that God would speedily advance his kingdom on the earth?

2. Alternately, the idea that this time is far off in some distant future begs the question of when, if an outpouring of prayer is to precede the fall of antichrist, God's people should actually commence such praying. Moreover, if they know when he is going to fall, why bother with such prayers, since God has fixed his fall at a certain date? What is Edwards's point in the two lines of argument reviewed in questions 1 and 2?

3. How might someone try to respond to Edwards's teaching, from Jesus and the Book of Daniel, that it is not for us to know the details or the time of the final events of history? Why does Edwards find it important to his proposal (for united, extraordinary prayer for revival) to defend the biblical teaching?

4. Just so we understand what he's saying, and why, what seems to be Edwards's point in all this argument about Constantine?

5. Psalm 126 is a psalm anticipating renewal in the Lord and counseling us how we should prepare for it—through envisioning such a time, and greatly longing for it (vv. 1–3); weeping tears of repentance as we plead with God to restore us (v. 4); and sowing the Word of God in hope of the Lord's blessing (vv. 5–6). How much of what you see in this psalm characterizes your life at this time? Your church? Take the time to pray through this psalm now.

❊ *Chapter 10* ❊

THE FALL OF ANTICHRIST MUST BE FAR OFF (2)

Edwards continues his rebuttal of Mr. Lowman's interpretation of Revelation and begins a discussion of the fall of mystical Babylon, as he presses his argument against the objection that the fall of antichrist is yet far off.

Constantine was the instrument of giving a mortal wound to the heathen Roman empire; and giving it a mortal wound in its *head,* namely, the heathen emperors then reigning, Maxentius and Licinius. But more eminently was this glorious change in the empire owing to the power of God's word, the prevalence of the glorious gospel, by which *Constantine* himself was converted, and so became the instrument of the overthrow of the heathen empire in the east and west.

ANOTHER HISTORICAL PROBLEM REBUTTED

The change that was then brought to pass, is represented as the destruction of the heathen empire, or the old heathen world; and therefore seems to be compared to that dissolution of heaven and earth that shall be at the day of judgment (Rev. 6:12, etc.). And therefore well might the heathen empire under the head which was then reigning, be represented as wounded to death (Rev. 13:3). It is much more likely that the wound the beast had by a sword in his head (Rev. 13:14), was the wound the heathen empire had in its head by that sword which (Rev. 1:16; 19:15) proceeds out of the mouth of Christ, than the wound that was given to the *Christian* empire and emperor by the sword of the heathen *Goths*. It is more likely that this wound was by that sword with which Michael made war with him, and overcame him, and cast him to the earth (Rev. 12:9) and that the deadly wound was given him at that very time. It is most likely that the sword which gave him this deadly wound, after which he strangely revived, as though he rose from the dead, was the same sword with that which shall at last utterly destroy him, so that he shall never rise more (Rev. 19:15, 19–21). This wounding of the head of the beast by the destruction of the heathen empire, and conversion of the emperor to the Christian truth, was a glorious event indeed of divine providence, worthy to be so much spoken of in prophecy. It is natural to suppose that the mortal wounding of the head of that savage cruel beast, represented as constantly at war with the woman, and persecuting the church of Christ, should be some relief to the Christian church; but on the contrary, that wounding to death Mr. Lowman speaks of, was the victory of the enemies of the Christian church *over her*, and the wound received *from them*.

It is said of that head of the empire that shall be next after the sixth head, and next before antichrist, and that is not reckoned as properly one of the number of the heads of the beast, that "when it comes, it shall continue a short space" (Rev. 17:10). By which we may understand, at least, that it shall be one of the shortest, in its continuance, of the successive heads. But the government seated at Ravenna, in the hands of the Goths, or of the deputies of the Greek emperors (which Mr. Lowman supposes to be meant by the head), continued, as Mr. Lowman himself takes notice, very near three hundred years. And if so, its continuance was one of the longest of the heads mentioned.

Besides, if the government Rome was under, from the time that Augustulus abdicated to the time when the pope was confirmed in his temporal dominion, was meant by the *seventh* head that was to be *between* the imperial head and the papal, there would doubtless have been *two* different heads mentioned, instead of one, between the emperor and the pope, namely, the first *Gothic* princes, who reigned one hundred years. Second, the *exarchs* of Ravenna, who governed for about one hundred and eighty-five years. The *Gothic* kingdom was much more properly a *district* government from the imperial, than the exarchate of *Ravenna*. For during the exarchate, *Rome* was under the government of the emperor, as much as it was in *Constantine's* time.

A Historical Inaccuracy
Rebutted

In Revelation 17:12 it is said, the "ten horns are ten kings, which are to receive power as kings one hour with the beast," or (as Mr. Lowman says it ought to have been translated) *the same hour* or *point of time with the beast.* This will not allow the time when antichrist first receives power as king to be so late as Mr. Lowman supposes. This division of the empire into many kingdoms, denoted by the number *ten,* was about the year four hundred and fifty-six, after *Genesericus* had take the city of *Rome:* but Mr. Lowman places the beginning of the reign of the antichrist in the year seven hundred and fifty-six, which is three hundred years later. I know, such an expression as *in one hour,* or *the same hour,* may allow of some latitude; but surely not such a latitude as this. This is a much longer time than it was from the time of the vision to *Constantine;* much longer than the space of all the first six seals; longer than it was from Christ's ascension to *Constantine;* and near as long as the time of all the reigns of the heathen emperors put together, from *Augustus Caesar* to *Constantine.* An hour is everywhere else in this book used to signify a very short time; as may be seen in places cited in the margin. And the expression, *the same hour,* everywhere else in the Bible, intends near the same point of time. The phrase *one hour* is used several times in the next chapter, speaking of the downfall of antichrist; and in each evidently signifies *a very short space of time.* And there is no reason why we should not understand the same phrase in the same sense, when used here concerning the rise of antichrist.

However, I do not deny that the time when Mr. Lowman supposes the reign of the beast began, even the time when *Pepin* confirmed to the pope his temporal dominions in Italy, was a time of the great increase and advancement of the power of antichrist in the world, and a notable *epoch*. And if I may be allowed humbly to offer what appears to me to be the truth with relation to the rise and fall of antichrist; it is this: As the power of antichrist, and the corruption of the apostate church, rose *not at once,* but by SEVERAL NOTABLE STEPS and degrees; so it will IN THE LIKE MANNER FALL: and that DIVERS STEPS and SEASONS OF DESTRUCTION to the spiritual Babylon, and revival of the true church, are prophesied of under ONE. And yet it may be true that there is some particular event, which prevails above all others in the intention of the prophecy, some remarkable season of the destruction of the church of Rome, the papal power and corruption, and advancement of true religion.

THE DESTRUCTION OF THE GREAT BABYLON

There are, as I apprehend, good reasons to hope that the work of God's Holy Spirit which in its progress will overthrow the kingdom of antichrist, and in its issue destroy *Satan's* visible kingdom on earth, will begin in a like time. The prophecy of the sixth vial (Rev. 16:12–16), if we take it in its connection with the other vials, and consider those providential events by which the preceding vials have manifestly been fulfilled, I humbly conceive, affords just ground for such a hope.

Vials of God's wrath on antichrist

It is very plain, from this whole chapter, as also the preceding and following, that all these seven vials are vials of God's wrath on *antichrist*; one is not poured out on the *Jews*, another on the *Turks*, another on *pagans*, another on the church of *Rome*; but they all signify God's successive judgments or plagues on the beast and his kingdom, which is in this chapter, and almost everywhere in this book, called GREAT BABYLON. And therefore undoubtedly, when it is said, "The sixth angel poured out his vial on the river *Euphrates*, and the water thereof was dried up, that the way of the kings of the east might be prepared," by the river *Euphrates* is meant something some way appertaining to this mystical *Babylon*; as the river *Euphrates* appertained to the literal *Babylon*. And it is very manifest that in the prophecy of this vial there is an allusion to that by which the way was prepared for the destruction of *Babylon* by Cyrus. This was done by turning the channel of the river *Euphrates*, which ran through the midst of the city. Hereby the way of the kings of the east, the princes of *Media* and *Persia*, was *prepared* to come in, under the walls of the city, at each end, and to destroy it; as they did that night wherein *Daniel* interpreted the hand-writing on the wall, against *Belshazzar* (Dan. 5:30).

A spiritual interpretation of the drying up of the Euphrates

The prophecies of *Babylon's* destruction, from time to time, take notice of this way of destroying her, by drying up the waters of the river *Euphrates,* to prepare the way for her enemies: "That saith to the deep, Be dry, and I will dry up thy rivers; that saith of *Cyrus,* he is my servant, and shall perform all my pleasure" (Isa. 44:27–28). "One post shall run to meet another, to show the king of *Babylon* that his city is taken at one end, and that the passages are stopped, and the reeds they have burnt with fire, and the men of war are affrighted" (Jer. 51:31, 23). And "I will dry up her sea, and make her springs dry" (Jer. 51:36). The *Medes* and the *Persians,* the people that destroyed *Babylon,* dwelt to the *eastward* of *Babylon,* and are spoken of as coming from the *east* to her destruction: "Calling a ravenous bird from the *east;* the man that executeth my counsel, from a far country" (Isa. 46:11). And the princes that joined this ravenous bird from the east, in this affair of destroying *Babylon,* are called *kings:* "The Lord hath raised up the spirit of the *kings* of the *Medes;* for his device is against *Babylon* to destroy it" (Jer. 51:11). "Prepare against her the nations, with the *kings* of the *Medes,* the captains thereof, and the rulers thereof" (Jer. 51:28). The dying of the channel of the river *Euphrates,* to *prepare the way* for these kings and captains of the east, to enter into that city, under its high walls, was the last thing done by the besiegers of *Babylon,* before her actual destruction. In like manner, the sixth is the last vial but one of God's wrath on the mystical *Babylon;* and the effect of it is the drying up of the channel, the last thing done against it before its actual destruction by the seventh vial. This opens the way for those who fight in a spiritual war against it, speedily to bring on its ruin.

Hence I think it may without dispute be determined that by the river *Euphrates* in the prophecy of this vial, is meant something appertaining to the mystical *Babylon*, or the *anti-Christian* church and kingdom, that serves it, in a way answerable to that in which the river *Euphrates* served old *Babylon*, and the removal of which will in like manner prepare the way for the enemies to destroy her. And therefore what we have to do in the first place, in order to find out what is intended by the river *Euphrates* in this prophecy, is to consider how the literal *Euphrates* served old *Babylon*. And it may be noted that *Euphrates* was of remarkable benefit to that city in two respects: it served the city as a *supply;* it was let through the midst of the city by an artificial canal, and ran through the midst of the palace of the king of *Babylon;* that part of his palace called the *old palace,* standing on one side, and the other part called the *new palace,* on the other; with communications from one part to another, above the waters, by a bridge, and under the waters, by a vaulted or arched passage; that the city, and especially the palace, might be plentifully supplied with water. Another way that the waters of *Euphrates* served *Babylon,* was as an *impediment* and *obstacle* in the way of its enemies, to hinder their access to destroy it. For there was a vast moat around the city, without the walls, of prodigious width and depth, filled with the water of the river, to hinder the access of her besiegers: and at each end of the city, the river served instead of walls. And therefore when *Cyrus* had dried up the river, the moat was emptied, and the channel of the river under the walls left dry; and so his way was prepared.

The meaning of Euphrates (1)

Therefore it is natural to suppose that by *drying up the waters* of the river *Euphrates*, in the prophecy of the destruction of the new *Babylon*, to prepare the way of her enemies, is meant the drying up of her *incomes* and *supplies*; and the removal of those things which hitherto have been the chief *obstacles* in the way of those who in this book are represented as at war with her, and seeking her destruction (Rev. 19:11, to the end, and Rev. 12:7), those things which have hindered their progress and success, or have been the chief *impediments* in the way of the protestant religion.

The first thing is the drying of the streams of wealth, the temporal supplies, revenues, and vast incomes of the *Romish* church, and the riches of the popish dominions. *Waters* in Scripture language very often signify *provision* and *supplies*, both temporal and spiritual. The temporal supplies of a people are very often in Scripture called waters: "Therefore my people is gone into captivity, and their honorable men are famished, and their multitude dried up with thirst," i.e., deprived of the supports and supplies of life (Isa. 5:13). And the drying up of the waters of a city or kingdom, is often used in Scripture prophecy for depriving them of their *wealth*, as the Scripture explains itself: "His spring shall become dry, and his fountain shall be dried up;

he shall spoil the treasure of all pleasant vessels" (Hos. 13:15). "The waters of Nimrim shall be desolate; for the hay is withered; the grass faileth; there is no green thing. Therefore the abundance they have gotten, and that which they have laid up, shall they carry away to the brook of the willows" (Isa. 15:6–7). The *brook of the willows* seems to refer to the waters of *Assyria* or *Chaldea,* whose streams abounded with willows (cf. Ps. 137:2). So that the carrying away of the treasures of *Moab,* and the adding of them to the treasures of *Assyria,* is here represented by the figure of turning away the waters of *Nimrim* from the country of *Moab,* and adding them to the waters of *Assyria,* as the prophecy explains itself.

Yea, even in the prophecies of the destruction of *Babylon* itself, the depriving of her treasures, seems to be one thing intended by the drying up of her waters. This seems manifest by the words of the prophecy in Jeremiah 50:37–38: "A sword is upon her treasures, and they shall be robbed; a drought is upon her waters, and they shall be dried up." Compare with Jeremiah 51:13: "O thou that dwellest upon many waters, abundant in treasures," [and] with Jeremiah 51:36, "I will dry up her sea, and make her springs dry."

The wealth, revenues, and vast incomes of the church of *Rome,* are the *waters* by which that *Babylon* has been nourished and supported; these are the waters which the popish clergy and members of the *Romish* hierarchy thirst after, and are continually drinking down, with insatiable appetite; and they are waters that have been flowing into that spiritual city like a great river; ecclesiastical persons possessing a very great part of the popish dominions. Accordingly, this *Babylon* is represented as vastly rich, in the prophecy of the *Apocalypse,* especially in the seventeenth and eighteenth chapters. These are especially the waters that supply the palace of the king of this new *Babylon,* namely, the pope; as the river *Euphrates* ran through the midst of the palace of the king of old *Babylon.* The *revenues* of the pope have been like *waters of a great river,* coming into his palace, from innumerable fountains, and by innumerable lesser streams.

STUDY QUESTIONS

1. Edwards's animus against the Roman Catholic Church of his day may be somewhat off-putting, and could possibly, at least for today's readers, derail his proposal. But let's take a step back from the historical and ecclesiastical specifics of Edwards's association of the Roman Church with the Babylon of Revelation. Let's look at some of the specifics of his complaint against it: it was greedy for power, identified earthly territory with rule, craved wealth, and overindulged in material resources. If Edwards had not been so specific in his use of the name of the Roman Catholic Church, might it be possible for us today to identify another church or churches that might fit that description?

2. Moreover, let's remember that Edwards is still arguing against thinking that the day of antichrist is still long off, and so it makes no sense to pray for his speedy downfall. He is trying to show that antichrist's power has been erod-

ing steadily for years. Look at 1 John 2:18–25. How does John define "antichrist" in this passage? What are the characteristics of antichrist?

3. In John's day the ratio of total world population to Christians was hundreds to one. In our day it is more like five to one. In John's day the church was poor and oppressed, owned no property, and had almost no political power. In our day the church has great wealth and is the most generous in charitable giving every year; church buildings and Christian enterprises abound. Given such comparisons, and keeping Edwards's argument in mind (about the "by stages" decline of antichrist), and remembering that John said that antichrist was already in the world in his day, should we be encouraged that Edwards's point is a valid one, his animus toward Rome notwithstanding? Why? How should this affect our response to his proposal for prayer?

4. Review the five psalms we have been using as prayers to guide us in revival. Going back to the work you did at the end of chapter 7, how might you work these five psalms, together with the work you did in chapter 7, into a proposal of your own?

5. Review the goals you set for this study. Are you making progress? In what way(s)?

Chapter 11

THE FALL OF ANTICHRIST MUST BE FAR OFF (3)

Edwards brings to a conclusion his argument about the Euphrates drying up, showing that since the things symbolized in this prophecy have already begun, then the fall of antichrist is already proceeding by stages, and the climactic revival of religion that precedes his final demise cannot be far off.

❖

THE PREVIOUS ARGUMENT EXTENDED

This prophecy[1] represents to us two cities very contrary the one to the other, namely, *New Babylon* and the *New Jerusalem,* and a river running through the midst of each.

New Jerusalem and New Babylon compared

The *New Jerusalem,* which signifies the church of Christ, especially in her best estate, is described as having "a river

1. He means the latter chapters of Revelation.

running through the midst of it" (Rev. 22:1–2). This river, as might easily be made most evident by comparing this with abundance of other Scriptures, undoubtedly signifies the *divine supplies;* the rich and abundant spiritual incomes and provisions of that holy city. Mr. Lowman, in his exposition, says, *It represents a constant PROVISION for the comfortable and happy life of all the inhabitants of this city of God.* And in his notes on the same place, he observes, "Water (says he) as necessary to the support of life, and as it contributes in great cities, especially in hot eastern countries, to the ornament of the place, and delight of the inhabitants, is a very proper representation of the enjoyment of all things, both for the support and pleasure of life." As the river that runs through the new *Jerusalem,* the church of Christ, refreshing that holy spiritual society, signifies their spiritual supplies, to satisfy their spiritual thirst; so the river that runs through the new *Babylon,* the *anti-Christian* church, that wicked carnal society, signifies, according to the opposite character of the city, her worldly, *carnal supplies,* to satisfy their carnal desires and thirstings.

The new *Jerusalem* is called in this book the *Paradise of God;* and therefore it is represented as having the tree of life growing in it (Rev. 2:7; 22:2). And it being described, as though a river ran through the midst of it, there seems to be some allusion to the ancient paradise in *Eden,* of which we are told that there ran a river through the midst of it to water it (Gen. 2:10), i.e., to supply the plants of it with nourishment. And this river was this very same *Euphrates,* which afterwards ran through *Babylon.* And in one and the other, it represented the divers *supplies* of two opposite cities. In *Eden*, it represented the *spiritual supplies* and wealth of the true Christian church, in her spiritual advancement and glory (Rev. 22:1–2). In the other, it represented the outward *carnal supplies* of the false *anti-Christian* church, in her worldly pomp and vain glory (Rev. 16:12).

The meaning of Euphrates (2)

When the waters that supply this mystical *Babylon* come to be dried up in this sense, it will prepare the way for *the enemies of anti-Christian corruption* that seek her overthrow. The *wealth* of the church of *Rome,* and of the powers that support it, is very much its *defense.* After the streams of her revenues and riches are dried up, or very greatly diminished, her walls will be as it were broken down, and she will become weak and defenseless, and exposed to easy ruin.

As the river *Euphrates* served the city *Babylon* for *supply;* so, as before observed, it served as an *impediment* or *obstacle* to hinder the access of its enemies: for there was a vast moat around the city, filled with the water of the river, which was left empty when *Euphrates* was dried up. And therefore we may suppose that another thing meant by the effect of the sixth vial, is the removal of those things which hitherto have been the *chief obstacles* to the progress of true religion, and the victory of the church of Christ over her enemies. These have been the corrupt *doctrines* and *practices* which have prevailed in protestant countries, the *doubts* and *difficulties* that attend many doctrines of the true religion, and the many *divisions* and *contentions* that subsist among protestants. The removal of these would wonderfully prepare the way for Christ and his armies to go forward and prevail against their enemies, in a glorious propagation of the true religion.

So that this vial, which is to prepare the way for Christ and his people, seems to have respect to that remarkable *preparing of the way* for Christ, by *leveling mountains, exalting valleys, drying up rivers,* and *removing stumbling-blocks,* which is often spoken of in the prophecies, as what shall precede the church's latter-day glory: "The Lord shall go forth as a mighty man; he shall stir up jealousy as a man of war; he shall prevail against his enemies. I will make waste mountains and hills, and dry up all their herbs; and I will make the rivers islands, and I will dry up the pools; and I will bring the blind by a way that they know not, and I will lead them in paths that they have not known; I will make darkness light before them, and crooked things straight: these things will I do unto them, and forsake them" (Isa. 42:13, etc.). "Prepare ye the way of the Lord; make straight in the desert a highway for our God: every valley shall be exalted, and every mountain and hill shall be made low, and the crooked shall be made straight, and the rough places plain; and the glory of the Lord shall be revealed, and all flesh shall see it together" (Isa. 40:3–5). "And the Lord shall utterly destroy the tongue of the *Egyptian* sea, and with his mighty wind shall he shake his hand over the river, and shall smite it in the seven streams thereof, and make men go over dry-shod: and there shall be an highway for the remnant of his people which shall be left from *Assyria,* like as it was to *Israel,* in the day that he came out of the land of *Egypt*" (Isa. 11:15–16). "Cast ye up, cast ye up, prepare the way, take up the stumbling-block out the way of my people" (Isa. 57:14). And, "Go through, go through the gates; prepare ye the way of the people; cast up, cast up the highway; gather out the stones; lift up a standard for the people" (Isa. 62:10). "I will bring them again also out of the land of *Egypt,* and gather them out of *Assyria;* and I will bring them into the land of *Gilead* and *Lebanon;* and place shall not be found for them. And he shall pass through the sea with affliction, and shall smite the waves of the sea; and all the deeps of the river shall dry up; and the pride of *Assyria* shall be brought down, and the scepter of *Egypt* shall depart away: and I will strengthen them in the Lord, and they shall walk up and down in his name, saith the Lord" (Zech. 10:10–12).

SUMMARY AND CONCLUSION OF THIS POINT

And it is worthy to be remarked that as *Cyrus* destroying *Babylon,* letting go God's captives from thence, and restoring *Jerusalem,* is certainly typical[2] of Christ's destroying mystical *Babylon,* delivering his people from her tyranny, and gloriously building up the spiritual *Jerusalem* in the latter days; so God preparing *Cyrus's* way, by drying up the river *Euphrates,* is spoken in similar terms, to signify the preparing of Christ's way, when he shall come to accomplish the latter event. Thus God says concerning *Cyrus,* "I will go before thee, and *make crooked places straight*" (Isa.

2. That is, a symbolic foreshadowing.

45:2). And, "I will direct, or make straight (as it is in the margin) all his ways" (Isa. 45:13). This is like Isaiah 40:2, 4, "Prepare ye the way of the Lord; make straight in the desert a highway for our God. The crooked things shall be made straight." "I will make darkness light before them, and crooked things straight" (Isa. 42:16).

It is true, we do not know how long this vial may continue running, and so Christ's way preparing, before it is fully prepared: but yet, if there be reason to think the effect of this vial is begun, or is near, then there is reason also to think that the beginning of that great work of God's Spirit, in the revival of religion, which, before it is finished, will issue in antichrist's ruin, is not far off. For it is pretty manifest that the *beginning* of this work will accomplish the *sixth* vial. For the gathering together of the armies of both sides, on the side of Christ and antichrist, to that great battle that shall issue in the overthrow of the latter, will be under this vial (cf. Rev. 16:12–14 with Rev. 19:11, to the end). And it is plain that Christ manifesting himself, wonderfully appearing, after long hiding himself, to plead his own and his people's cause, and riding forth against his enemies in a glorious manner—and his people following him in pure linen, or *the practice of righteousness and pure religion*—will be the alarm to antichrist, and cause him to gather that vast host to make the utmost opposition. But this alarm and gathering together is represented as being under the sixth vial. So that it will be a great *revival,* and a mighty *progress* of true religion under the sixth vial, eminently threatening the speedy and utter overthrow of *Satan's* kingdom on earth, that will so mightily rouse the old serpent to exert himself with such exceeding violence, in that greatest conflict and struggle that ever he had with Christ and the church, since the world stood.

All the seven vials bring terrible *judgments* upon antichrist, but there seems to be something distinguishing by the three last, the *fifth, sixth,* and *seventh,* namely, *that they more directly tend to overthrow his kingdom;* and accordingly, each of them is attended with a great reviving of religion. The *fifth* vial was attended with such a revival and reformation, as greatly weakened and diminished the *throne* or kingdom of the beast, and went far toward its ruin. It seems as though the *sixth* vial should be much more so; for it is the distinguishing note of this vial that it is the *preparatory,* which more than any other vial *prepares the way* for Christ's coming to destroy the kingdom of *antichrist,* and to set up his own kingdom in the world.

Besides, those things which belong to the *preparation of Christ's way,* so often represented by leveling mountains, drying up rivers, etc., namely, *unraveling intricacies, and removing difficulties attending Christian doctrines; distinguishing between true religion and its false appearances; detecting and exploring errors and corrupt principles; reforming the wicked lives of such professors,* which have been the chief stumbling-blocks and obstacles that have hitherto hindered the progress of true religion: these things are the proper work of the Spirit of God, promoting and advancing divine light and true piety,[3] and can be the effect of nothing else.

3. For Edwards on just how this occurs, see the first volume in this series, *Growing in God's Spirit* (Phillipsburg, N.J.: P&R, 2003).

And that the *beginning* of that glorious work of God's Spirit, which shall finally bring on the church's latter-day glory, will accompany that other effect of this vial—turning the streams of the wealth of the world, bringing its treasures, and the gains of its trade and navigation, into the true protestant church of Christ—seems very manifest, because this very effect is spoken of as that which shall be at the beginning of this glorious work: "Who are these that fly as a cloud, and as doves to their windows? Surely the isles shall wait for me, and the ships of Tarshish, *first,* to bring thy sons from far, their silver and gold with them, unto the name of the Lord thy God, and to the Holy One of Israel, because he hath glorified thee" (Isa. 60:8–9). So that it is to be hoped that before this effect, now probably begun, is at an end, the Spirit of God will so *influence the hearts of the protestants* that they will be disposed to devote to the service of God the silver and gold they take from their popish enemies, and the gains of their trade and navigation, both to the *East* and *West Indies,* so that *their merchandise and hire shall be holiness to the Lord.*

Agreeably to what has been supposed, that an extraordinary outpouring of the Spirit of God is to accompany this *sixth* vial; so the beginning of a work of extraordinary awakening has already attended the probable beginning of it, continued in one place or other for many years past: although it has been, in some places, mingled with much enthusiasm, after the manner of things in their first beginnings, unripe, and mixed with much crudity. But it is to be hoped a far more pure, extensive, and glorious revival of religion is not far off, which will more properly be the beginning of that work which in its issue shall overthrow the kingdom of antichrist and of *Satan* through the world. But God *will be inquired of for this, by the house of* Israel, *to do it for them.*

If, notwithstanding all I have said, it be still judged there is sufficient reason to determine that the ruin of antichrist is at *a very great distance;* and if all I have said—as arguing that the beginning of the glorious revival of religion, which in its continuance and progress will destroy the kingdom of antichrist, is not very far off—be judged to be of no force; yet it will not follow that our complying with what is proposed to us in the late *Memorial* from *Scotland,* will be in vain, or not followed with such spiritual blessings, as will richly recompense the pains of such extraordinary prayer for the Holy Spirit, and the revival of religion. If God does not grant that greatest of all effusions of his Spirit, so soon as we desire; yet we shall have the conscious satisfaction of having employed ourselves in a manner that is certainly agreeable to Christ's will and frequent commands—in being much in prayer for this mercy, much more than has heretofore been common with Christians—and there will be all reason to hope that we shall receive some blessed token of his acceptance. If the fall of mystical *Babylon,* and the work of God's Spirit that shall bring it to pass, be at several hundred years' distance; yet, it follows not that there will be no happy *revivals of religion* before that time, which shall be richly worth the most diligent, earnest, and constant prayer.

STUDY QUESTIONS

1. Whew! That was a long way to get to the point of the final section of this chapter. What *is* Edwards's point in all this discussion of the Euphrates drying up?

2. The Protestant Reformation, the advance of Protestantism, and recent great awakenings of true religion would have been for Edwards signs that antichrist was losing his grip on the world. Look again at some of the terms he uses to describe antichrist: "wicked carnal society," "worldly pomp and vain glory," "false appearances" of true religion, and so forth. As a child of his era Edwards would have naturally equated such things with Roman Catholic Christianity of his day. In other settings he will say almost as much about deists and Arminians (though not with such strong language). It seems clear that if forced to speak in the abstract only, Edwards would argue that antichrist is best embodied in worldly religion, as John indicated in 1 John 2. What would be some contemporary examples of the spirit of antichrist afoot in the world?

3. Do you see any indications that this spirit is "losing its grip" on the world? What evidence do you see of the "drying up" of the "Euphrates" of contemporary false religion? Do you think that true Christians are making the most of

this opportunity to "go under the walls," as it were, and bring down the house of false religion? Why or why not?

4. How might an extraordinary, united effort at prayer for revival help to hasten the demise of false religion and its ability to mislead and captivate so many people? What effect might such an effort have in your community?

5. Suppose you wanted to take up Edwards's proposal and organize an effort to pray for revival: Based on all we've seen and discussed thus far, what would such a proposal include? See if you can write in no more than two or three sentences what you propose. Now, to whom would you take this proposal in order to get something started in your church?

❈ Chapter 12 ❈
SUCH PRAYER IS A NOVELTY

Edwards shows by Scripture and historical precedent that the objection that such a proposal for prayer is but a novelty is without base.

❈

I would say something to one objection more, and then hasten to the conclusion of the discourse. Some may be ready to object that what is proposed in this *Memorial* is a *new thing,* such as never was put in practice in the church of God before.

THIS ALREADY A COMMON PRACTICE

If there be something *circumstantially* new in it, this cannot be a sufficient objection. The duty of *prayer* is no new duty. For many of God's people expressly to agree, as touching *something they shall ask* in prayer, is no new thing. For God's people to agree on circumstances of *time and place* for united prayer, according to their own discretion, is no new thing. For *many,* in *different places,* to agree to offer up *extraordinary prayers* to God, at the *same time,* as a token of their union, is no new thing; but has been commonly practiced in the appointment of days of fasting and prayer for special mercies. And if the people of God should engage in the duty of prayer for the coming of Christ's kingdom, in a *new manner*—that they resolve not to be so negligent in this duty, as has been common with professors of religion heretofore, but will be more frequent and fervent in it— this would be such a new thing as *ought* to be, and would be only to *reform a former negligence.* And for the people of God in various parts of the world, visibly, and by express agreement, to *unite* for this extraordinary prayer, is no more than their duty; and no more than what it is foretold the people of God should *actually* do, before the time comes of the church's promised glory on earth. And if this be a *duty,* then it is a duty to come into some *method* to render this *practicable:* but it is not practicable (as was shown before) but by *this method,* or some other equivalent.

This Method of Prayer Not New

And as to *this particular method,* proposed to promote union in extraordinary prayer—God's people in various parts setting apart fixed seasons, to return at certain periods, wherein they agree to offer up their prayers at the same time—it is not so new as some may possibly imagine. This may appear by what follows; which is a part of a paper, dispersed abroad in *Great Britain* and *Ireland,* from *Lon-*

don, in the year 1712, being the latter end of Queen *Anne's* reign, and very extensively complied with, entitled, "A serious call from the city to the country, to join with them in setting apart some time, namely, from seven to eight every Tuesday morning, for the solemn seeking of God, each one in his closet, now in this so critical a juncture—Jonah 1:6, 'Call upon God, if so be that God will think upon us, that we perish not.' " What follows is an extract from it:

"You have formerly been called upon to the like duty, and have complied with it; and that not without success. It is now thought highly seasonable to renew the call. It is hoped that you will not be more backward, when it is so apparent that there is even greater need. It is scarce imaginable how a professing people should stand in greater need of prayer, than we do at this day. You were formerly bespoke from that very pertinent text, Zechariah 8:21: 'The inhabitants of one city shall go to another, saying, Let us go speedily to pray before the Lord (or, as the marginal reading, more expressive of the original reading, is) continually, from day to day, to entreat the face of the Lord.' According to this excellent pattern, we of this city, the metropolis of our land, think ourselves obliged to call upon our brethren in *Great Britain* and *Ireland,* at a time when our hearts cannot but meditate terror, and our flesh tremble for fear of God, and are afraid of his righteous judgments: those past being for the most part forgotten; and the signs of the times foreboding evil to come, being by the generality little, if at all, regarded: we cannot therefore but renew our earnest request, that all who make conscience of praying for the peace of *Jerusalem*, who wish well to *Zion*, who would have us and our posterity a nation of *British* protestants, and not of popish bigots and *French* slaves, would give us (as far as real and not pretended necessity will give leave) a meeting at the throne of grace, at the hour mentioned; there to wrestle with God, for turning away his anger from us, for our deliverance from the hands of his and our enemies, for turning the councils of all *Ahitophels*, at home and abroad, into foolishness; for mercy to the queen and kingdom; for a happy peace, or successful war so long as the matter shall continue undetermined; for securing the protestant succession in the illustrious house of *Hanover* (by good and evil wishes to which, the friends and enemies of our religion and civil rights are so essentially distinguished), and especially for the influences of divine grace upon the rising generation, particularly the seed of the righteous, that the offspring of our Christian heroes may never be the plague of our church and country. And we desire that this solemn prayer be begun the first Tuesday after sight, and continued at least the summer of this present year, 1712. And we think every modest, reasonable, and just request, such as this, should not on any account be denied us; since we are not laying a burden on others, to which we will not most willingly put our own shoulders; nay, indeed, count it much more a blessing than a burden. We hope this will not be esteemed by serious protestants, of any denomination, a needless step; much less do we fear being censured by any such, as fanciful and melancholy, on account of such a proposal. We with them believe a providence, know and acknowledge that our God is a God hearing prayer. Scripture recordeth, and our age is not barren of instances, of God's working marvelous deliverances for his people in answer to humble, believing, and importunate prayer; especially when prayer and reformation go together; which is what we desire. Let this counsel be acceptable to us, in this day of our church's calamity, and our common fears. Let us seek the Lord while he may be found, and call upon him while he is near. Let us humble ourselves under the mighty hand of God. Let us go and pray unto our God, and he will hearken unto us. We shall seek him and find him, when we search for him with all our hearts. Pray for the peace of *Jerusalem*: they shall prosper that love her. And may *Zion's* friends and enemies both cry out with wonder, when they see the work of God; Behold they pray! What hath God wrought! Verily there is a God that judgeth in the earth.

"*Postscript*. It is desired and hoped, that if any are hindered from attending this work at the above-mentioned hour, they will nevertheless set apart an hour weekly for it."

God speedily and wonderfully heard and answered those who were united in that extraordinary prayer, in suddenly scattering those black clouds which threatened the nation and the protestant interest with ruin, at that time; in bringing about, in so remarkable a manner, that happy change in the state of affairs in the nation, which was after the queen's death, by bringing King *George* the First, just at the time when the enemies of the religion and liberties of the nation had ripened their designs to be put in speedy execution. And we see in the beginning of this extract that what is proposed, is mentioned as being no new thing, but that God's people in *Great Britain* had *formerly* been called upon to like duty, and had complied, not without *success*. Such agreements have several times been proposed in *Scotland*, before this which is now proposed to us; there was a proposal published for this very practice, in the year 1712, and another in 1735. So that it appears this objection of *novelty* is built on a mistake.

STUDY QUESTIONS

1. Review the extract from the proposal of 1712 that Edwards quoted in this section. Does this extract suggest any ways you might want to fine tune the proposal you drew up at the end of the last chapter? Compare what you wrote there with this extract, to see how you might improve your proposal.

2. What objections to taking up Edwards's proposal yet linger in you? If you were challenged to be part of an effort of united, extraordinary prayer for revival, what would keep you from agreeing to it?

3. How do you think Edwards might try to argue you out of your objections?

4. Meet with your prayer partner to review the psalms we have been using to pray for revival during this study. Choose one or two of them, and use them to guide your time together in prayer.

5. Below, make a list of the individuals and groups in your church you plan to challenge to take up this proposal for extraordinary prayer according to the proposal you have drafted. Then, beside each name, put a date when you plan to contact that person or group.

❊ Chapter 13 ❊

Concluding Considerations

Edwards concludes his discourse by pleading with the readers not to reject or neglect so reasonable a proposal, and calling them to persevere in this effort.

Now, upon the whole, I desire every serious Christian who may read this discourse, calmly and deliberately to consider, whether he can excuse himself from complying with what has been proposed to us, and requested of us, by those ministers of Christ in *Scotland*, who are the authors of the late *Memorial*.

One Part of the Church Calling to Another to Seek God's Mercies

God has stirred up a part of his church, in a distant part of the world, to be in an extraordinary manner seeking and crying to him that he would appear to favor *Zion*, as he has promised. And they are applying themselves to us, to join with them; and make that very proposal to us, which is spoken of in my text, and in like manner and circumstances. The members of one church, in one country, are coming to others in distant countries, saying, *Let us go speedily and constantly to pray before the Lord, and to seek the Lord of hosts.* Will it not become us readily to say, *I will go also?* What these servants of Christ ask of us, is not silver or gold, or any of our outward substance, or that we would put ourselves at any cost, or do anything that will be likely to expose us to remarkable trouble, difficulty, or suffering in our outward interest; but only that we would help together with them, by our prayers to God, for the greatest mercy in the world; a mercy which as much concerns us as them; for the glory of their Lord and ours; for the great advancement of our common interest and happiness, and the happiness of our fellow-creatures, through all nations; a mercy, of which, at this day especially, there is great need; a mercy, which we, in this land, do stand in particular need of; a mercy, which the word of God requires us to make the subject matter of our prayers above all other mercies, and gives us more encouragement to pray earnestly and unitedly to him for, than any other mercy; and a mercy, which the providence of God toward the world of mankind, at this day, loudly calls the people of God to pray for. I think we cannot reasonably doubt but that these ministers have acted a part becoming disciples of the great Messiah, and ministers of his kingdom; and have done the will of God, according to his word, in setting forward such an affair at this day, and in proposing it to us. And therefore, I desire it may be considered, whether we shall not really sin against God, in refusing to comply with their proposal and request, or in neglecting it, and turning it by, with but little notice and attention; therein disregarding that which is truly a call of God to us.

This Proposal the Work of Honest Gentlemen

The ministers that make this proposal to us, are no separatists or schismatics; are no promoters of public disorders, nor of any wildness or extravagance in matters of religion; but are quiet, peaceable members and ministers of the church of *Scotland,* who have lamented the late divisions and breaches of that church. If any shall say, they cannot judge of their character, but must take it on trust from others, because they conceal their names; in answer to this, I would say, that I presume no sober person will say that he has any reason to suspect them to be any other than gentlemen of honest intention. Be assured, there is no appearance of anything else but an upright design in their proposal; and that they have not mentioned their names, is an argument of it.

It may well be presumed, from the manner of their expressing themselves in the *Memorial* itself, that they concealed their names from what perhaps may be called an excess of modesty; choosing to be at the greatest distance from appearing to set forth themselves to the view of the world, as the heads of a great affair, and the first projectors and movers of something extraordinary. And therefore, they are careful to tell us that they do not propose the affair, but as a thing already set on foot; and do not tell us who first projected it. The proposal is made to us in a very proper and prudent manner, with all appearance of Christian modesty and sincerity, and with a very prudent guard against anything that looks like superstition, or whatsoever might entangle a tender conscience. Far from any appearance of design to promote a particular party, or denomination of Christians, in opposition to others, with all appearance of the contrary, it is their charitable request that none would by any means conceive of any such thing to be in their view, and that all—of every denomination and opinion concerning the late religious commotions—would join them in seeking the common interest of the kingdom of Christ. And therefore, I think, none can be in the way of their duty in neglecting a proposal in itself excellent, and which they have reason to think is made with upright intentions, merely because the proposers modestly conceal their names. I do not see how any *serious* person, who has even an ill opinion of the late religious stirs, can have any color of reason to refuse a compliance with this proposal, on that account. The more disorders, extravagances, and delusions of the devil have lately prevailed, the more need have we to pray earnestly to God, for his Holy Spirit, to promote *true religion,* in opposition to the grand deceiver, and all his works. And the more such prayer as is proposed, is answered, the more effectually will all that is contrary to sober and pure religion be extirpated and exploded.

THE PROPOSAL A CAUSE
FOR REJOICING

One would think that each who favors the dust of *Zion*, when he hears that God is stirring up a considerable number of ministers and people to unite in extraordinary prayer, for the revival of religion and the advancement of his kingdom, should greatly *rejoice* on this occasion. If we lay to heart the present calamities of the church of Christ, and long for that blessed alteration which God has promised, one would think it would be natural to rejoice at the appearance of something in so dark a day, which is so promising a token. Would not our friends that were lately in captivity in *Canada,* who earnestly longed for deliverance, have rejoiced to have heard of anything that seemed to forebode the approach of their redemption? And particularly, may we not suppose such of them as were religious persons, would have greatly rejoiced to have understood that there was stirred up in God's people an extraordinary spirit of prayer for their redemption? I do not know why it would not be as natural for us to rejoice at the like hopeful token of the redemption of *Zion,* if we made her interest our own, and preferred *Jerusalem* above our chief joy.

LET US GO SPEEDILY TO PRAY

If we are indeed called of God to comply with the proposal now made to us, then let me beseech all who sincerely love the interest of real Christianity, notwithstanding any diversity of opinion and former disputes, to *unite*, in this affair, with one heart and voice: and *let us go speedily to pray before the Lord*. There is no need that one should wait for another. If we can get others our neighbors to join with us, and so can conveniently spend the quarterly seasons with praying societies, this is desirable; but if not, why should we wholly neglect the duty proposed? Why should not we perform it by ourselves, uniting in heart and practice, as far as we are able, with those who in distant places are engaged in that duty at that time?

If it be agreeable to the mind and will of God that we should comply with the *Memorial*, by praying for the coming of Christ's kingdom, in the manner therein proposed, then doubtless it is the duty of all to comply in that respect also, namely, in endeavoring, as far as in us lies, to *promote others joining in such prayer*, and to render this *union* and agreement as *extensive* as may be. Private Christians may have many advantages and opportunities for this; but especially ministers, inasmuch as they not only are by office overseers of whole congregations of God's people, and their guides in matters of religion, but ordinarily have a far more extensive acquaintance and influence abroad, than private Christians in common have.

And I hope that such as are convinced it is their duty to comply with and encourage this design, will remember we ought not only to go *speedily* to pray before the Lord, and to seek his mercy, but also to go *constantly*. We should unite in our practice these two things, which our Savior unites in his precept, PRAYING and NOT FAINTING. If we should continue some years, and nothing remarkable in providence should appear as though God heard and answered, we should act very unbecoming believers, if we should therefore begin to be disheartened, and grow dull and slack in seeking of God so great a mercy. It is very apparent from the word of God that he is wont often to try the faith and patience of his people, when crying to him for some great and important mercy, by withholding the mercy sought, for a season; and not only so, but at first to cause an increase in dark appearances. And yet he, without fail, at last succeeds those who continue instant in prayer with all perseverance, and "will not let him go except he blesses." It is now proposed that this extraordinary united prayer should continue for *seven years,* from *November* 1746. Perhaps some who appear forward to engage, may begin to think the time *long,* before the seven years are out; and may account it a dull story, to go on for so long time, praying in this extraordinary method, while all yet continues *dark* without any dawnings of the wished-for light, or appearance in providence of the near approach of the desired mercy. But let it be considered, whether it will not be a poor business, if our faith and patience is so short-winded that we cannot be willing to wait upon God for seven years, in a way of taking this little pains, in seeking a mercy so infinitely vast.

For my part, I sincerely wish and hope that there *may not be an end of extraordinary united prayer,* among God's people, for the effusions of the blessed Spirit, when the seven years are ended; but that it will be continued, either in this method, or some other, by a *new agreement* that will be entered into with greater engagedness, and more abundant alacrity, than this is; and that extraordinary united prayer for such a mercy will be *further propagated and extended,* than it can be expected to be in seven years. But, at the same time, I hope God's people, who unite in this agreement, will see some tokens for good before these seven years are out, that shall give them to see, God has not said to the seed of *Jacob,* Seek ye me in vain; and shall serve greatly to animate and encourage them to *go on in united prayers for the advancement of Christ's kingdom,* with increasing fervency. But whatever our hopes may be in this respect, we must be content to be ignorant of *the times and seasons,* which the Father hath put in his own power; and must be willing that God should answer prayer, and fulfill his own glorious promises, *in his own time;* remembering such instructions, counsels, and promises, of the word of God as these: "Wait on the Lord, be of good courage, and he shall strengthen thine heart; wait, I say, on the Lord" (Ps. 27:14). "For the vision is yet for an appointed time; but in the end it shall speak, and not lie: though it tarry, wait for it; because it will surely come, it will not tarry" (Hab. 2:3–4). "I will look unto the Lord, I will wait for the God of my salvation: my God will hear me" (Mic. 7:7). "God will wipe away tears from off all faces, and the rebuke of his people shall he take away from off all the earth; for the Lord hath spoken it. And it shall be said in that day, Lo, this is our God! We have waited for him, and he will save us; this is JEHOVAH! We have waited for him, we will be glad and rejoice in his salvation" (Isa. 25:8–9). Amen.

STUDY QUESTIONS

1. Summarize Edwards's "hopes" for this proposal. Are these your hopes as well?

2. You now have learned how you may use certain of the psalms to pray for revival. You have begun to unite with at least one other person to pray. And you have prepared a proposal that could be used to call others to join you in this effort. Which of these will you continue to pursue? Which will you let go? Why?

3. Have you realized the goals you set for yourself for this study? In what ways? Have any new goals come to mind?

4. Have you begun meeting with the people and groups you listed at the end of the last chapter, to challenge them to join you in this effort? What results are you seeing?

5. How might God use you to lead others to consider Edwards's proposal for united, extraordinary prayer for revival? Will you take up the challenge to do so?

Index of Scripture